L·190

AN ANVIL ORIGINAL
Under the general editorship of Louis L. Snyder

DEISM: AN ANTHOLOGY

PETER GAY
Professor of History
Columbia University

D1438404

D. VAN NOSTRAND COMPANY, INC.
PRINCETON, NEW JERSEY
TORONTO · MELBOURNE · LONDON

To
AUNT HATTIE

VAN NOSTRAND REGIONAL OFFICES
New York, Chicago, San Francisco

D. VAN NOSTRAND COMPANY, LTD., *London*
D. VAN NOSTRAND COMPANY (Canada), LTD., *Toronto*
D. VAN NOSTRAND AUSTRALIA PTY. LTD., *Melbourne*

COPYRIGHT, 1968, BY
PETER GAY
Published simultaneously in Canada by
D. VAN NOSTRAND COMPANY (Canada), LTD.

PRINTED IN THE UNITED STATES OF AMERICA

Preface

Deism is an intellectual movement that has been much neglected. This, I think, is unfortunate, for while the deists were not on the whole impressive philosophers, their thought was of great importance for the formation of the philosophy of the Enlightenment. It is the aim of this anthology to make available sizable excerpts from some of the major texts. Although most of these texts have been unavailable for many years, a few of them are now once more becoming obtainable in rather expensive reprints. Hence there is much point in offering these selections, and in giving each spokesman a good deal of room for expression. All the deists, after all, were polemicists—that is, men of the word, or rather, of many words—and it is only through a glimpse at these polemics that we can grasp the full meaning of the deist debate in the seventeenth and eighteenth centuries.

My procedure has been as follows: I have offered a general introduction to deism (Part I), which suggests the road to a full interpretation of the movement and says something about the environment in which the deists worked. Then (in Part II) I have introduced each selection with a sizable headnote which should help the reader find his way into the controversy. If this anthology sends the reader to a rare-book room to find the whole pamphlet of which I here offer a part, the anthology will have justified itself.

PETER GAY

Table of Contents

Part I

DEISM: INTRODUCTION

CHAPTER 1

Toward an Interpretation

The history of deism has usually been written as the history of a great debate—a debate the deists lost. The procedure seems reasonable, and the verdict just. From the end of the 1690s, when the vehement response to John Toland's *Christianity Not Mysterious* started the deist debate, to the end of the 1740s, when the tepid response to Middleton's *Free Inquiry* signalized its close, English divines, supported and goaded by passionate laymen, refuted the doctrines of the deist sect, elicited restatements of the deist position, and, with barely concealed pleasure, composed rebuttals. Each deist tract produced several answers, for there were few deists and many ambitious clerics, and in those years—the last years of the Stuarts and the first years of the Hanoverians—the road to preferment lay as much through polemics as through political subservience. The cleric who did not publish was likely to perish in some remote village, and he had every reason to be grateful to the deists, who offered inexhaustible material for the exercise of dialectical skill, sardonic wit, and pious indignation. Theological controversy had been the staple diet of the literate public since Elizabethan days, and serious religious questions had been widely, if somewhat delicately, argued. Then in 1694, just two years before Toland's book appeared, the Licensing Act was allowed to lapse, and while freedom of expression continued to be shackled by stringent laws of libel, including blasphemous libel, it became possible to touch on fundamental religious issues with only a modicum of caution. As the deists discovered to their regret, complete freedom of expression was indeed elusive, but they could say much with impunity, and more with adroit indirection—and so they said much, and developed techniques for implying more than they said. Silence, it seemed, was in the interest of no one, and for half a century a pamphlet war enlivened, almost dominated, the English scene. Hundreds of Englishmen broadcast their views on the fulfillment of the prophecies, the credentials of miracles, the organization of the primitive church, the morals of ecclesiastics, and the nature of Jesus Christ himself. The debate ended only after it had exhausted its subject, its participants, and, one suspects, its audience.

Deism, then, produced a great debate, and a debate the deists were bound to lose: the opposing side engrossed most of the talent. Among the deists, only Anthony Collins (1676-1729) could claim much philosophical competence; only Conyers Middleton (1683-1750) was a really serious scholar. The best known deists, notably John Toland (1670-1722) and Matthew Tindal (1656-1733) were talented publicists, clear without being deep, forceful but not subtle. "Toland and Tindal," Pope said of them, "prompt at priests to jeer." [1] Others, like Thomas Chubb (1679-1747), were self-educated freethinkers; a few, like Thomas Woolston (1669-1731), were close to madness. And even the sane among the deists had a paranoid view of history and politics: they saw conspiracies everywhere, conspiracies against reasonable philosophers in the past and religious reformers—themselves —in the present. Against the suave logic of Bishop Joseph Butler (1692-1752), the ruthless wit of Alexander Pope (1688-1744), the acute penetration of David Hume (1711-1776), they could muster only common sense, a healthy skepticism, some knowledge of religious history, some telling abuse, and a certain brutish, patient obsession with their polemics against "superstition."

Yet to see deism merely through its obvious manifestations, and to judge it merely by its immediate consequences, is to miss its significance in the development of the Western mind. It has often been noted, and it deserves to be noted again, that for most of his recorded history man has been a religious animal. After deism, and partly because of it, he was so no longer.[2] Obviously no one, least of all the deists, would make deism alone, or even chiefly, responsible for this mutation. Deism reflected and articulated a critical transition in religious consciousness, but by reflecting and articulating it so plainly, so coarsely, it hastened the transition. The impact of the deist polemic was felt wherever men

[1] *Dunciad,* II, 399 and note.
[2] See especially, Roland N. Stromberg, *Religious Liberalism in Eighteenth-Century England* (1954).

reasoned about religion. The secular Enlightenment, which was by no means dominated by deists, is the deists' rightful heir.

This claim—and it is a far-reaching claim—raises important questions: just how clearly did the deists see their historic role? precisely how radical were they? The deists themselves rather differed on the answers to these questions. Partly from caution but also partly from conviction, many of them liked to describe themselves as Christians, indeed as the only true Christians of their day, while a few gloried in their distance from that "old superstition." But the deists' adversaries did not hesitate: Calvinists and Arminians might denounce one another as erring brethren; Protestants and Catholics might call one another children of Anti-Christ. But there was in these denunciations a sense that all alike were struggling for the same symbols; all alike, after all, were claiming the exclusive right to speak for the same faith. These mutual hatreds, though often deep and usually vicious, were the hatreds of true competitors playing the same game. The deists, on the other hand, were outside this game; they had no place in the consensus of Christian conflict. "The Deists," Jonathan Edwards wrote, "wholly cast off the Christian religion, and are professed infidels. They are not like the Heretics, Arians, Socinians, and others, who own the Scriptures to be the word of God, and hold the Christian religion to be the true religion, but only deny these and these fundamental doctrines of the Christian religion: they deny the whole Christian religion." True, "they own the being of God; but deny that Christ was the son of God, and say he was a mere cheat; and so they say all the prophets and apostles were: and they deny the whole Scripture. They deny that any of it is the word of God. They deny any revealed religion, or any word of God at all; and say that God has given mankind no other light to walk by but their own reason." [3] However much other Christians might differ from Edwards in detail, the general outlines, and the profound horror, of Edwards' denunciation were almost universally shared. The deists, everyone said, were impious innovators, aliens in a Christian society rudely trampling on all that men held sacred. To remote observers, the distance between radical Protestants

[3] *History of the Works of Redemption,* in *The Works of President Edwards,* 4 vols. (1857), I, 467.

and deists might seem negligible, but to contemporaries it was decisive. It made all the difference if one accepted revelation, no matter how attenuated, or the Christian God, no matter how remote, or rejected both revelation and the Christian God altogether. The deists might be religious men, but in their natural religion, nature was primary and religion evaporated.

But whatever the judgment of contemporaries, modern historians have generally acted the part of the remote observer, with some gain in objectivity, perhaps, but also much loss of comprehension. The deists, these modern historians have declared, only said what others thought, learned all their techniques from their Christian neighbors, only pushed radical Protestant doctrine a single step farther. "If Protestantism was unintentionally acting as a screen for rationalism," Sir Leslie Stephen writes, "rationalism naturally expressed itself in terms of Protestantism." [4] Suspicious of breaks in history and fond of continuities, most historians have followed Sir Leslie and argued that to isolate deism among the intellectual currents of late-seventeenth- and early-eighteenth-century England is to distort it.

Now these historians have an important point. But so did the deists' contemporaries. The relation of deism to its environment and its predecessors was in fact a dialectical one; it was intimate and remote. The deists were disciples who learned what they could and then rejected their preceptors. If it is true that the deists took only a single step, it is also true that the step they took was across an unbridgeable abyss.

This dialectic has been unintentionally concealed by Sir Leslie Stephen's celebrated distinction between constructive and critical deism, a distinction that most historians have accepted with only minor modifications. First, Sir Leslie argued, the constructive deists tried to substitute a natural religion and pagan morality for Christian doctrine; then the critical deists tried to prove the Christian story naïve, absurd, and oppressive. "The doubts as to the facts were preceded by the doubts as to the value of the established creed." [5] But this distinction, no matter how subtly

[4] Sir Leslie Stephen, *English Thought in the Eighteenth Century*, 2 vols. (3rd ed., 1902), I, 79.

[5] *Ibid.*, I, 93—but, with all my criticisms, I should pay tribute here to this great work. Stromberg, *Religious Liberalism*, is far from uncritically accepting of this distinction.

it may be presented, obscures more than it clarifies. All deists were in fact both critical and constructive deists. All sought to destroy in order to build, and reasoned either from the absurdity of Christianity to the need for a new philosophy or from their desire for a new philosophy to the absurdity of Christianity. Each deist, to be sure, had his special competence. While one specialized in abusing priests, another specialized in rhapsodies to nature, and a third specialized in the skeptical reading of sacred documents. Yet, whatever strength the movement had— and it was at times formidable—it derived that strength from a peculiar combination of critical and constructive elements. Deism, we might say, is the product of the confluence of three strong emotions: hate, love, and hope. The deists hated priests and priestcraft, mystery-mongering, and assaults on common sense. They loved the ethical teachings of the classical philosophers, the grand unalterable regularity of nature, the sense of freedom granted the man liberated from superstition. They hoped that the problems of life—of private conduct and public policy— could be solved by the application of unaided human reason, and that the mysteries of the universe could be, if not solved, at least defined and circumscribed by man's scientific inquiry. The deists were optimists about human nature: they rejected the Fall and thought that man could be at once good and wise. Had they only hated, they would have been cranks. Had they only loved, they would have been enthusiasts. Had they only hoped, they would have been visionaries. They were something of all this, but since they combined these qualities, they were something more and something better as well. They were powerful agents of modernity.

CHAPTER 2

The Deist Environment

1. The Political Situation. Toward the end of the seventeenth century, when deism first emerged as a serious intellectual position, the Western world was actively freeing itself from its medieval heritage. Experience contradicted time-honored explanations, and so new explanations became not merely possible but fashionable. Men, educated and uneducated alike, were still Christians, and many were still deeply devout. Only a few scandalous outsiders, philosophers like Thomas Hobbes (1588-1679) or Baruch Spinoza (1632-1677), taught—or could be interpreted to teach—atheism. Only a few rakes spouted blasphemies and swinish Epicurean maxims. But these lost souls were isolated in their salons; they made converts only among their few peers. Yet, while the world remained religious, religion was in flux. The Copernican hypothesis had found wide acceptance; in the days of Toland one could certainly be a good Copernican and a good Christian at the same time. But the displacement of the earth from the center of the universe did have some unsettling religious implications. It was threatening news to some, delightful news to many, but important news to all who could think. Natural philosophers, physicists, and astronomers had been making astounding discoveries for a century. They had discovered the Milky Way, the moons of other planets, spots on the sun, and universal forces holding the solar system together. More than that, natural philosophers had devised and were eloquently advocating new intellectual methods, methods of inquiry designed to lead to new discoveries, to produce agreement among learned investigators and thus avoid fatiguing wrangles about mere words. As one could be a good Copernican and a good Christian, so in the late seventeenth century one could be a good Newtonian and a good Christian as well—the clergymen who flocked to the Royal Society demonstrated that. However, the new teachings in physics and astronomy, and scientific method in general, compelled serious reconsideration of just what it meant to be a good

Christian—and just how a good Christian might possess the essentials of his creed while discarding the adventitious. For several centuries, travelers and explorers had reported on new civilizations (not always very accurately) and had found enormous audiences for their books: travel ranked second only to theology in popularity among the reading public. But by the end of the seventeenth century, the travel literature, like the scientific literature, was becoming a threat to accepted convictions; it was acquiring the status of moral and even theological criticism. If there were advanced cultures, guided by ethical philosophies as pure as any the Christian world had to offer, and if these cultures could be shown never to have heard of Christ, what then became of the exclusive claims of the Christian dispensation? American Indians could be written off as savage children of the devil, but the Chinese, about whom the Jesuits wrote back glowing reports, could not be disposed of this simply. The Chinese, it seemed, were a sage people, who studied the admirable writings of Confucius, subjected their public servants to stringent and rational examinations, and conducted their political and social affairs with a minimum of strain and hateful persecution. China was a vast argument in behalf of cultural relativism, and cultural relativism was a threat to the Christian view of the world.

Beyond this, the classics of Greece and Rome—chiefly of Rome—had been stripped of their medieval incrustations and misinterpretations in the Renaissance, and as early as the fifteenth century Italian humanists had used the writings of Cicero and Tacitus, Seneca and Horace, to modify and partly to discredit the Christian theology of their day. But most of the humanists had remained within the Christian fold. By the seventeenth century, the classics became even more radical, more dissolvent, than they had been in the Renaissance. In the hands of a few writers, they became guidebooks to rebellion against the God-given social order. Thomas Hobbes testifies to this—and Hobbes is a good witness, for he was not a very religious man and held no brief for religious justifications of political obedience. "As to rebellion in particular against monarchy," he wrote, "one of the most frequent causes of it, is the reading of the books of policy, and histories of the ancient Greeks, and Romans. . . .

From the reading, I say, of such books, men have undertaken to kill their kings." [6] Clearly, wherever one looked—to science, to travel, to the classics—the intellectual ferment of the seventeenth century had political consequences.

Indeed, it was political through and through. The overwhelming realities of the day, to which all these intellectual currents contributed and which they served, were the persistence of religious division and the growth of the modern secular state. In the sixteenth century it had still seemed possible to Catholic enthusiasts that the Protestant heresy might be wiped from the face of the earth, like earlier heresies—while Protestant enthusiasts for their part could hope that the Whore of Babylon, now reigning in Rome, might be banished back to hell whence she had sprung. And the ideal of religious unity had been championed by men less violent than these: in the midst of abuse of unprecedented brutality and of frightful religious civil war, irenic spirits had prayed for the reunion of all Christian churches.

But by the end of the seventeenth century, both the rage of the bellicose majority and the hope of the pacific minority remained unfulfilled. It was becoming obvious—even to statesmen, who are often the last to see obvious things—that Protestantism and Catholicism would somehow have to coexist, on the same continent and in the same country. It is easy for us today to deplore the bigotry and the myopia of the men who refused to accept these realities, but when Louis XIV revoked the Edict of Nantes in 1685 and drove thousands of French Huguenots into exile or underground, and when Anglican divines refused to countenance schemes for comprehension that would have given dissenting Protestants a place in the Church of England, both the French king and the English clerics were acting on impulses and convictions that had characterized European civilization for many centuries.

Self-righteousness is an almost inescapable concomitant of dogmatic religion: if there is only one truth and one way to the truth, then dissenters must be not merely mistaken but wicked, not merely unfortunate but eternally damned, not merely absurd but a threat to society. Toleration was a radical idea, an in-

[6] See *Leviathan*, chapter 29.

novation confronting an age that feared innovations, thundered against them, and introduced them daily.

But the grounds of intolerance were beginning to shift. In his celebrated *Letter Concerning Toleration* (1689), John Locke (1632-1704) urged the exclusion of those who arrogated to themselves the right to depose their king by excommunication and those who "deny the being of a God." Roman Catholics and atheists were unacceptable, even to Locke who was a radical in his time, because the first were agents of a foreign power and the second could not be trusted on oath. In a word, the grounds for intolerance or limited tolerance, at least for Locke, were political rather than religious. Locke's way was the recognition of present realities and the way of the future; it arose from a new secular conception of politics. In this view, the state is a legal entity rather than a religious community; the task of the state is not to school men for salvation but to maintain public order at home and power abroad. In this new state, the duties of the subject are to keep the peace, pay his taxes, and do whatever share of the public business (if any) falls to him. To be sure, men continued to be religious, kings continued to be fanatical, clergymen continued to seek power. But some sort of toleration, both in the national and international sphere, was becoming a practical necessity even if it was theoretically defended by only a few advanced philosophers. Medieval political philosophy, which was essentially a philosophy for a tribe, was becoming irrelevant to the political situation of the seventeenth century, and Christian thinkers found it necessary to come to terms with a world that had changed out of all recognition.

2. The Religious Response. There was nothing new in the need for compromise. From its beginnings, and through its long career in the world, the history of Christianity has been the history of great compromises. I am not suggesting that these compromises were deliberate political arrangements devised by shrewd ecclesiastical statesmen. This charge has long been a favorite with the critics of Christianity, and the deists resorted to it freely. But it is psychologically implausible and historically false. The great compromises—between reason and revelation, mystical experience and orderly church government, the classics and the Scriptures, asceticism and worldliness—were sometimes noble, sometimes pathetic attempts to preserve two cherished values that were in tension with one another. St. Augustine was a trained rhetorician and an admirer of Plato, and he never wholly surrendered his affection either for rhetoric or for Platonism. (Why give up either if both could be preserved in an embracing scheme of piety?) St. Thomas Aquinas was a rationalist and an Aristotelian. (Should it not be possible to approach God through reason and to follow Aristotle's arguments at least part of the way?) With the Renaissance—still, despite its reputation, overwhelmingly religious—these questions became even more pressing than they had been before. The candid appreciation of classical writings without Christian reinterpretations, the admiration of classical beauty in art and literature, the careful study of classical philosophy, put Renaissance philosophers under severe pressure, and led them into some astonishing contortions. The very title of Marsilio Ficino's great work, *Theologia Platonica,* suggests the lengths to which the humanists felt themselves compelled to go in their search for a synthesis between classical culture and Christian doctrine.

The Protestant Reformation at first tried to do away with the need for such compromises. Luther and Calvin, and after them their followers, insisted that they were returning to the pure piety and pure practice of primitive Christianity.[7] But, then, what precisely *was* pure, primitive Christianity? Neither the word of Scriptures, nor the practice of the early Christians, nor the treatises of the much-admired Church Fathers were wholly unambiguous. As the English Puritans discovered, not even the question of ecclesiastical organization could be resolved by a simple appeal to Holy Writ. The Presbyterians found justification there for one type of church polity, the Congregationalists for another, and in the same texts. All Protestants were sure that they were uncompromising Christians, but their uncompromising Christianity varied from sect to sect and, in the radical Reformation, from man to man. As Roman Catholics constantly warned,

[7] There is some irony in this nostalgia. Even if they had succeeded in returning to "primitive" Christianity, they would have returned to a set of beliefs that was itself not "pure"—Christianity from the very beginning was a conflation (or a synthesis) of Jewish religious ideas, Greek philosophical notions, and Oriental cult practices.

not without satisfaction and not without justification, the Protestants' disdainful rejection of authoritative tradition and an authoritative priesthood, and the appeal to private judgment, inevitably spawned sects and endless theological disagreement. Besides, the exercise of private judgment permitted the Protestant not so much to avoid as to conclude compromises: he could come to terms with the new ideas around him.

Nor was this all. The passage of time, the intrusion of the world, the discoveries of the new philosophy (to which Protestants in general responded enthusiastically), forced Protestants into some painful confrontations with modernity. New England, a laboratory for Puritan asceticism, where the saints had things pretty much their own way for many years, demonstrated that pure Christianity was impossible to maintain without concessions to the world. And in Europe, the flexibility of at least some Protestants compelled other adjustments. It was from this modern Protestantism that the deists would draw most of their intellectual and polemical arsenal.

The religious situation of the late sixteenth and the seventeenth century was extremely complicated. The most significant strands in the tapestry of reform were four: the simple piety of the *politiques* and their allies; the optimistic piety of the Arminians; the philosophical piety of the Cambridge Platonists; and the reasonable piety of the Latitudinarians.

Simple Piety. Since the days of Erasmus, a handful of radical but influential intellectuals had sought for a short catalogue of Christian dogmas, a list of beliefs that all intelligent Christians must believe and could agree upon. Some of these writers were mystics searching for some ineffable religious truth to which all could repair and which would make persecution unnecessary; others, like Montaigne, poured the acid of skepticism alike on the rage to believe and the rage to persecute. By the early seventeenth century, the call for simple Christian piety was echoed most effectively by the Christian Stoics, by scholars like Justus Lipsius (1547-1606), who sought to reconcile the teachings of ancient Stoicism with their own Christianity to produce a credible religion.

Optimistic Piety. Joined to this effort to find the essentials of the Christian faith in a few believable and incontrovertible state-

ments was the optimistic piety developed mainly in the rising
Dutch Republic by Jacobus Arminius (1560-1609) and his
followers. Arminius repudiated the harsh doctrine of Grace
preached by Augustine and taught that all men might deserve
heaven. His sermons offended the rigid Calvinists in his country
as in other countries, but there was something almost irresistible
about Arminius' sermons, in which God was a God of Love and
Christian conduct an inner reformation that might lead men to
eternal bliss.

Philosophical Piety. The Dutch Arminians were in close touch
with a small group of English divines, the Cambridge Platonists.
Benjamin Whichcote (1609-1683), Ralph Cudworth (1617-
1688), and Henry More (1614-1687) sought to go beyond the
dogmas that divide the faithful to the philosophical bases that
might unite them. They inveighed against "enthusiasm" and instead extolled the role of rational inquiry in religion. Without
doubt they were pious men, and nothing was further from their
thought than the overthrow of traditional Christian beliefs. But
they insisted that it was possible to discover, by the pious use
of reason, which of these beliefs were essential, which mere
accretions. The Cambridge Platonists, John Tulloch has written,
were truly "religious philosophers" who "sought to marry philosophy to religion, and to confirm the union on the indestructible basis of reason and the essential elements of our higher
humanity." [8]

Reasonable Piety. All these efforts, which had their beginning
with the devout humanism of Erasmus, found their culmina-
tion in the preaching of the English Latitudinarians. This group
of orthodox and powerful divines, who dominated the Church of
England in the second half of the seventeenth and the first half
of the eighteenth century, would have been horrified if attention had been called to the aid they were giving the deists. But
the aid was there. John Tillotson (1630-1694), who ended his
long and distinguished career as Archbishop of Canterbury,
preached his elegant influential sermons to appreciative audiences and influenced both the rhetorical and the theological
style of generations of Churchmen. Tillotson, in essence, taught

[8] John Tulloch, *Rational Theology and Christian Philosophy in England in the Seventeenth Century,* 2 vols. (1872), II, 13-14.

that God's burden on man was light, that man was made for salvation and eternal bliss, and that he might achieve his divinely-ordained purposes by relatively simple means. Man did not need to believe the "nonsense" imported into Christianity by the Romans; he ought not to engage in emotional outbursts: God had given man reason and good sense that he might exercise them freely and fully, in the sphere of religion as much as elsewhere. It was comforting doctrine and fully in accord with the philosophical revolution then under way.

3. The Philosophical Revolution. The philosophical and the scientific revolutions of the seventeenth century were one and the same, and it was essentially this great revolution, though not led by deists, that gave rise to modern deism. It began with Bacon, Galileo, and Descartes early in the century: it produced such mavericks as Hobbes and Spinoza; and it culminated in the writings of Newton and Locke at the end of the century.

Bacon, Galileo, Descartes. It is fashionable to pit Bacon, the prophet of empiricism, against Descartes, the pioneer of modern rationalism—and both Bacon and Descartes, the philosophers, against Galileo, the superb practitioner. Differences in emphasis, mood, and even philosophy certainly existed among these three men, but from a larger perspective it is clear that they were allies. All, each in his own way, were the philosophical prophets of the new science. All agreed with Bacon's ambitious formulation: mankind must do nothing less than undertake "a total reconstruction of sciences, arts, and all human knowledge, raised upon proper foundations." [9] And it was the business of these thinkers to discover those proper foundations, for one thing was clear—these foundations had not been laid by the Scholastics or the philosophers of the Renaissance.

> The knowledge whereof the world is now possessed [Bacon insisted] especially that of nature, extendeth not to magnitude and certainty of works. The Physician pronounceth many diseases incurable, and faileth oft in the rest. The Alchemists wax old and die in hopes. The Magicians perform nothing that is permanent and profitable. The mechanics take small light from natural philosophy, and do but spin on their own little threads.[10]

[9] *The Great Instauration,* in *Works,* IV, 8.
[10] *Filium Labyrinthi,* in *ibid.,* III, 496.

What was needed, therefore, was not a new discovery, or even a host of new discoveries, but a new method. And that method, Bacon said, and Galileo and Descartes said with him, was the method of the sciences: the mixture of mathematical intuition and laborious empirical enquiry, the fashioning of mechanical and intellectual instruments that would enable the researcher to probe more deeply into the mysteries of nature than had been possible before and (which was more significant) to develop a systematic intellectual procedure that would enable successive generations of scientists to confirm and correct the findings of their predecessors. Bacon, Galileo, and Descartes sought to make science cumulative and self-correcting.

This was essential work for the deists, for, despite their own intentions, the scientific revolutionaries threw doubt on most of the accepted stories of Christianity. They did so neither directly nor deliberately. But they were developing a method that would construct a body of knowledge on which all men could agree—and if there was anything certain in the world, it was that theologians did not agree, and could not agree, and would never agree.

Hobbes and Spinoza. In the midst of this revolution, a number of intellectuals turned quite directly to the claims of the theologians and pronounced them all unproved, unprovable, and probably false. Some of these radicals were modern Epicureans, citing their favorite text, Lucretius' *De rerum natura.* These had little influence. But there were also two thinkers of stature, Hobbes and Spinoza, despised and rejected—and read.

Thomas Hobbes (1588-1679) is a complicated and in some respects a shadowy figure: the precise nature of his own religious beliefs remains a matter of some dispute. But it is clear that his influence was on the side of disbelief, and it is certain that the deists learned much from him. "The philosopher of Malmesbury," Bishop Warburton wrote in the eighteenth century, "was the terror of the last age, as Tindal and Collins are of this." [11] He might have added that the terrors of his own day were much indebted to their illustrious predecessor.

Hobbes himself argued steadfastly that he believed in a God,

[11] Quoted in John Orr, *English Deism: Its Roots and Its Fruits* (1934), 79.

and that reason would discover him to any man ready to trust his reason. There are even occasional—very occasional—passages in which he speaks of the truths of revelation and the "blessed Savior Jesus Christ." But for the most part, his God is a remote and philosophical figure, and, while his writings against the Roman Catholic Church—"the Kingdom of Darkness"—are cast in the approved style of Protestant polemics against Papists, his specific teachings on the credibility (or rather incredibility) of tales of revelation gave good Protestants little comfort and earned him the reputation of an atheist. It was not so much that Hobbes openly denied the possibility of revelation; it was, rather, that in his persuasive epistemological writings he managed to throw doubt on nearly all the methods that Christians had used to proclaim that a revelation had taken place. If a man claims, for instance, that God has revealed something to him, there is no way for him to prove that the revelation is genuine; if he claims that the revelation came to him in a dream, this means no more than that a man dreamed that God had spoken to him. "So that though God Almighty can speak to a man by dreams, visions, voice, and inspiration; yet he obliges no man to believe he hath done so to him that pretends it; who, being a man, may err, and, which is more, may lie." [12] Here was a prescription for skepticism that the deists would take up, at interminable length, in the decades after Hobbes's death.

Beyond this, Hobbes raised some difficult questions both as to the authorship and the authenticity of the Scriptures. Clearly —and here too the deists would read him with great profit— the Church that had long been dominant in Europe had been corrupt, mendacious, power-hungry, and Reformers had effectively demolished many of their incredible tales of miracle-working saints and divinely blessed relics. How much more, Hobbes asked, might not a reasonable man do with, or to, the miracles that remained? It was an uncomfortable question.

Hobbes raised other questions, equally uncomfortable. In some remarkable pages of his *Leviathan,* he offered a natural history of the religious sentiment, and concluded that the "natural seed of religion" consisted of "opinion of Ghosts, ignorance of second causes, devotion toward what men fear, and taking of things

[12] *Leviathan,* chapter 32.

casual for prognostics." [13] In essence, this was an ancient procedure: the Greeks had already speculated on the reason why
men were religious. But Hobbes went beyond them to offer a
brilliant, if incomplete, psychological account of the religious
impulse; nothing among the many subversive things he did was
more subversive than this.

Hobbes was a master of the English language, and constantly
enmeshed in controversy. Spinoza wrote as a rigorous mathematical logician, chiefly in Latin, and his influence was therefore
less marked than Hobbes's. Yet he too became notorious as an
atheist, and his writings were required reading for radicals in his
time—most of whom did not read him well. But while the pantheism of his *Ethics* (1677) had to await the late eighteenth
century before it was clearly seen and fully appreciated, the
theological position of his *Theological-Political Treatise* (1670)
was perfectly transparent from the beginning. The *Treatise* is a
prescient masterpiece of the higher criticism, written long before scholars had, as it were, invented this discipline. Spinoza
points out that once the Bible is confronted as any other book
is confronted—as a book written by human authors and subject
to the ordinary canons of consistency—it becomes evident that
it is not the work of a single, but the work of many hands, and
that many tales, especially the tales of miracles, are interpola-
tions into earlier stories. In the *Ethics,* Spinoza had indicated
his conviction that there could be no miracles, because God
(who is nature) does not violate the laws of which He is Himself an embodiment; in the *Treatise,* Spinoza indicates just how
the reports of miracles were written and inserted into the holy
text. It was a fruitful hypothesis, and the deists made the best
of it.

Newton and Locke. Neither Isaac Newton (1642-1727) nor
John Locke (1632-1704) was a deist, yet both were indispen-
sable to the deist cause. Newton gathered the scattered laws of
physics and astronomy into a single imposing system, and while
there was room in that system for divine intervention—God,
Newton thought, set the universe right once in a while when it
threatened to run down—the Newtonians could safely disregard
this kind of theology as a personal idiosyncrasy. What mattered

[13] *Ibid.,* chapter 12.

was that the regularity of the universe had been reduced to system and, in a modest way, explained. What mattered, also, was that Newton did not merely embody the empirical method of the sciences, he also wrote about it with conviction, and convincingly. "I do not feign hypotheses" (*Hypotheses non fingo*), he wrote in a much-quoted pronouncement. He refused to go beyond the evidence; he rejected systems that must be spun out of the head of the ambitious philosopher; he relied upon experiment, observation, and mathematical generalization alone. This was, as I have said, not a deist tenet, but it encouraged men to move in the direction of deism: Newton's prestige as a sage— the world's greatest man, as Voltaire admiringly called him—lent weight to speculations in which miracles, supernatural interventions, and priestcraft, had no place.

It was, finally, in the work of Locke that the groundwork of deism was completed. Locke was above all an empiricist: man acquires knowledge by his sensations upon which his reflection plays. He achieves authentic certainty only in the way of the "natural philosopher," which is to say, the scientist. In his great *Essay Concerning Human Understanding* (1690), Locke drew the consequences of this position: revelation is but reason extended; if it is anything else, if it subverts or contradicts reason, it is not authentic revelation, but a deception.

Yet Locke in his own way was a Christian, though he was sharply criticized for being something less, and something worse, in his own time. *"The Reasonableness of Christianity"* (a book Locke had published in 1695), "and *Christianity not Mysterious,"* (the deist book Toland published in the following year), "these two Titles," a critic wrote in 1706, "are different in Sound, but agree in Sense." [14]

There we are back at the beginning. That critic was both right and wrong. Locke, in the *Reasonableness of Christianity,* had driven the call for a simple, an optimistic, a philosophical, and a reasonable piety, to as great lengths as it would go: he indicated that all a Christian need believe—but this he must believe—is that Christ is the Messiah. This was not much; it was too little for most Christians. But it was not yet deism. In this sense, the critic

---

[14] William Carroll, quoted in John W. Yolton, *John Locke and the Way of Ideas* (1956), 178.

was wrong. But in the sense that it was indeed too little for most Christians, and that while the step from Locke to Toland was across an abyss it was still only a single, and not very surprising step, the critic was right. Liberal Protestantism was not deism, but it helped to make deism inevitable.

Part II

READINGS

A. THE PRECURSORS

READING NO. 1

De veritate*

Edward, Lord Herbert of Cherbury

Edward, Lord Herbert of Cherbury (1583-1648), has long been called "the father of deism." The title is as just as such titles can ever be: his general view of religion had been anticipated by such classical philosophers as Cicero, but in his own time, Herbert was the first to move away from Christian Stoicism or liberal Protestantism to develop a religious philosophy that needs no special revelation. Herbert had a versatile career: he was a soldier as much as he was a philosopher, a diplomat as much as he was a poet, but it is for his deist work, De veritate, *published in Paris in 1624, and for his* Autobiography *(first published in 1886), which is marked by some revealing passages, that he is best known.*

De veritate *is important for deism not merely in the beliefs it seeks to defend, but also, and more, for the theory of knowledge it advocates—or rather for the prominence that theory of knowledge has in Herbert's religious speculations. Herbert's point may seem obvious, but it became obvious only after thinkers like him had stated it, over and over again: because there is such rabid disagreement in religious matters, the only road to reliable religious conviction is through the study of the conditions and possibilities of knowledge. Accordingly, Herbert opens* De veritate *with chapters on "The General Conditions and Definition of Truth," "The Conditions of Perception," and so forth, before he turns to the question of revelation. The chapter on "Common Notions concerning Religion" (from which I have printed extensive excerpts below), was of great importance to Herbert, and*

* The following selection is taken from Chapters IX and X of Herbert's *De veritate,* translated and edited by Meyrick H. Carré (1937), pp. 289-313, with Mr. Carré's kind permission.

*acquired considerable notoriety. It is here that Herbert lists the
famous "five notions" which make up the true religion. But, as
Meyrick H. Carré has pointed out, it was generally "forgotten
that the Religious Common Notions were only the application
in one sphere of the theory of knowledge unfolded in the body
of the work."* [1] *From Herbert on, deism sought to rest its case,
explicitly or implicitly, on epistemological foundations.*

*For all his radicalism, Herbert was a characteristic seven-
teenth-century man in his mixture of rationalism and superstition, his longing for logical clarity and profound mystery. In his*
Autobiography, *he reports that he had severe doubts about publishing his* De veritate, *and, in his perplexity, he said a prayer:
"I had no sooner spoken these words, but a loud though yet
gentle noise came from the heavens, for it was like nothing on
earth,"* [2] *and Herbert took the noise as a divine encouragement.
It is important to remember the incident, if only to remember
that the seventeenth- and eighteenth-century minds, even of skeptics and scoffers, were far apart.*

COMMON NOTIONS CONCERNING RELIGION

. . . . Every religion which proclaims a revelation is not good,
nor is every doctrine which is taught under its authority always
essential or even valuable. Some doctrines due to revelation may
be, some of them ought to be, abandoned. In this connection the
teaching of Common Notions is important; indeed, without them
it is impossible to establish any standard of discrimination in
revelation or even in religion. Theories based upon implicit faith,
though widely held not only in our own part of the world but
also in the most distant regions, are here irrelevant. Instances of
such beliefs are: that human reason must be discarded, to make
room for Faith; that the Church, which is infallible, has the right
to prescribe the method of divine worship, and in consequence
must be obeyed in every detail; that no one ought to place such
confidence in his private judgment as to dare to question the
sacred authority of priests and preachers of God's word; that

---

[1] "Introduction," *De Veritate,* by Edward, Lord Herbert of Cherbury
(1937), 56.
[2] *Autobiography,* (ed. 1906), 133-4.

their utterances, though they may elude human grasp, contain so much truth that we should rather lay them to heart than debate them; that to God all the things of which they speak and much more are possible. Now these arguments and many other similar ones, according to differences of age and country, may be equally used to establish a false religion as to support a true one. Anything that springs from the productive, not to say seductive seed of Faith will yield a plentiful crop. What pompous charlatan can fail to impress his ragged flock with such ideas? Is there any fantastic cult which may not be proclaimed under such auspices? How can any age escape deception, especially when the cunning authorities declare their inventions to be heaven-born, though in reality they habitually confuse and mix the truth with falsehood? If we do not advance towards truth upon a foundation of Common Notions, assigning every element its true value, how can we hope to reach any but futile conclusions? Indeed, however those who endeavour to base their beliefs upon the disordered and licentious codes of superstition may protest, their behavior is precisely similar to people who with the purpose of blinding the eyes of the wayfarer with least trouble to themselves offer with singular courtesy to act as guides on the journey. But the actual facts are otherwise. The supreme Judge requires every individual to render an account of his actions in the light, not of another's belief, but of his own. So we must establish the fundamental principles of religion by means of universal wisdom, so that whatever has been added to it by the genuine dictates of Faith may rest on that foundation as a roof is supported on a house. Accordingly we ought not to accept any kind of religion lightly, without first enquiring into the sources of its prestige. And the Reader will find all these considerations depend upon Common Notions. Can anyone, I beg to ask, read the huge mass of books composed with such immense display of learning, without feeling scorn for these age-long impostures and fables, save in so far as they point the way to holiness? What man could yield unquestioning faith to a body which, disguised under the name of the Church, wastes its time over a multitude of rites, ceremonies, and vanities, which fights in so many parts of the world under different banners, if he were not led to perceive, by the aid of conscience, some marks of worship, piety, penance, reward and

punishment? Who, finally, would attend to the living voice of
the preacher if he did not refer all his deeds and words to the
Sovereign Deity? It would take too long to deal with every instance. It is sufficient to make clear that we cannot establish any
of them without the Common Notions. I value these so highly
that I would say that the book, religion, and prophet which ad-
heres most closely to them is the best. The system of Notions,
so far at least as it concerns theology, has been clearly accepted
at all times by every normal person, and does not require any
further justification. And, first of all, the teaching of Common
Notions, or true Catholic Church, which has never erred, nor ever
will err and in which alone the glory of Divine Universal Providence is displayed, asserts that

There is a Supreme God.

No general agreement exists concerning the Gods, but there is
universal recognition of God. Every religion in the past has acknowledged, every religion in the future will acknowledge, some
sovereign deity among the Gods. . . . Accordingly that which
is everywhere accepted as the supreme manifestation of deity, by
whatever name it may be called, I term God. I pass on to consider
His attributes, using the same method. And in the first place I
find that He is Blessed. Secondly, He is the end to which all
things move. Thirdly, He is the cause of all things, at least in so
far as they are good. From which follows, according to His
Providence that, in the fourth place, He is the means by which
all things are produced; for how could we pass from the beginning to the end but by the means provided? We need not be
deterred by the type of philosophers who have refused to grant
the medium any share of providence. Since circumstances seldom
fall out in accordance with their wishes, they make a desperate
attempt to abolish particular Providence as though the course
of events were ordained by themselves and not by the Divine
will. We must realise that writers of this kind are only wrangling
about the means by which Divine Providence acts; they are not,
I think, disputing Providence itself. Meanwhile the utmost agreement exists concerning Universal Providence, or Nature. But
every religion believes that the Deity can hear and answer
prayers; and we are bound to assume a special Providence—to

omit other sources of proof—from the universal testimony of
the sense of divine assistance in times of distress. In the fifth
place, He is eternal. For we are taught by a Common Notion
that what is first is eternal. In the sixth place a Common Notion
tells us that the Deity is good, since the cause of all good is
supremely good. In the seventh place, He is just; a Common Notion, experience and history bear witness at every point that the
world is ruled under His Providence with absolute justice. For
as I have often observed, Common Notions, which solve the
most difficult questions of philosophy and theology, teach us that
all things are governed with righteousness and justice, though
their causes may be hidden from us. In the eighth place, He is
wise; for marks of His wisdom do not only appear in the attributes of which I have spoken, but are manifest daily in His
works.

In addition to these qualities there are certain attributes, such
as Infinity, Omnipotence and Liberty, concerning which I find
there is much difference of opinion. But His infinity is proved
by the infinity of position or space. For the supreme God pene-
trates all things, according to the teaching of Common Notions
His Omnipotence follows from His infinity, for it is certain that
there is nothing which is beyond the power of the infinite. His
omnipotence proves His liberty, since no man in his senses has
ever doubted that He who can do everything is absolutely free.
I think, however, that those who feel otherwise must be ap-
proached from a different angle. And here there is a Common
Notion that what exists in us in a limited degree is found absolutely in God. If He is so far beyond our capacity as to be illimit-
able He will be infinite. If He has created all things without using
any existing matter He will be omnipotent. And finally if He is
the Author of our liberty He will be supremely free. . . . The
Divine Attributes prove these points as effectively when taken
separately as when taken together. . . . It is true that I have
found that the names which they have given these attributes are
conflicting and often inappropriate. Thus the Pagans confuse the
attribute of infinity with that of unity, and invent a number of
Gods. Even if you suppose with some that under the names of
Apollo, Mars, and Ceres, various aspects of Divine Providence
were recognised, you cannot deny that the fables which the an-

cients invented under these names have always been thought foolish, since no one has ever doubted (so far as I am aware) the evils of their creed. As for the attributes which are rejected in our discussion, they are those which make the Deity strange, physical, composite, particular, or capable of condemning men for His own pleasure. Such a God is nothing but an idol of the imagination, and exists nowhere else. I pass now to the second Common Notion of theology.

This Sovereign Deity ought to be Worshipped.

While there is no general agreement concerning the worship of Gods, sacred beings, saints, and angels, yet the Common Notion or Universal Consent tells us that adoration ought to be reserved for the one God. Hence divine religion—and no race, however savage, has existed without some expression of it—is found established among all nations, not only on account of the benefits which they received from general providence, but also in recognition of their dependence upon Grace, or particular providence. Hence, too, men have been convinced, as I have observed above, that they can not only supplicate that heavenly Power but prevail upon Him, by means of the faculties implanted in every normal man. Hence, finally, what is a more important indication, this Power was consulted by the seers in order to interpret the future and they undertook no important action without referring to it. So far the peoples were surely guided by the teaching of Natural Instinct. The All Wise Cause of the universe does not suffer itself to be enclosed within its own sphere, but it bestows general Grace on all and special Grace on those whom it has chosen. Since everyone can experience this in himself, would it not be unjust to refuse the same power to God? God does not suffer us to beseech Him in vain, as the universal experience of divine assistance proves, to pass over all other arguments. Although I find that the doctrine of special providence, or Grace, was only grudgingly acknowledged by the ancients, as may be gathered from their surviving works, yet since the worship of the Divine Power was recognised in every age, and carried with it this doctrine of Grace or Special Providence, I assert that this doctrine is a Common Notion. From this source spring supplications, prayers, sacrifices, acts of thanksgiving;

to this end were built shrines, sanctuaries, and finally for this purpose appeared priests, prophets, seers, pontiffs, the whole order of ministers. And even if their activity has been equally evident in human affairs as in the affairs of God, since they have often been a crafty and deceitful tribe, prone to avarice, and often ineffective, this is because they have introduced much under the pretext of Religion which has no bearing upon Religion. In this way with extraordinary skill they have confused sacred matters with profane, truth with falsehood, possibility with probability, lawful worship with licentious ceremonies and senseless superstitions; with the result, I make bold to say, that they have corrupted, defiled, and prostituted the pure name of Religion. However necessary the priests were, whenever they brought contempt upon themselves, the fear of God and the respect due to sacred things diminished in proportion. Accordingly we must give them the honour which is due to them. I obtain, then, proof of this external aspect of divine worship in any type of religion from every age, country and race. It is therefore a Common Notion. It is no objection that temples or regions sacred to the Gods are not found among savages. For in their own fashion they consulted oracles and undertook no serious task without propitiating their Deity. . . . However, if anyone denies the assertion we must reply that the same religious faculties which anyone can experience in himself exist in every normal human being, though they appear in different forms and may be expressed without any external ceremony or ritual. And in postulating this principle I draw the conclusion that religion is the ultimate difference of man. I am not deterred by the fact that irreligious men exist, and even some who appear to be atheists. In reality they are not atheists; but because they have noticed that some people apply false and shocking attributes to God, they have preferred not to believe in God, than to believe in a God of such a character. When He is endowed with true attributes so far from not believing in Him they would pray that such a God might exist, if there were no such Being. If, however, you still maintain that irreligious persons and even atheists can be found (which I do not believe), reflect that there may be not a few madmen and fools included among those who maintain that rationality is the final difference of man. Otherwise there would hardly have been such endless disputes about Religion, nor such a multitude of martyrs; for there is no Church which does not boast of its legendary heroes, men who for the sake of religion have not only adopted lives of the utmost austerity, but have endured death itself. Such conflicts would not have occurred if there had not been men so stubborn and unreasonable that they were incapable of distinguishing truth from probability, possibility and falsity. . . .

The connection of Virtue with Piety, defined in this work as the right conformation of the faculties, is and always has been held to be, the most important part of religious practice.

There is no general agreement concerning rites, ceremonies, traditions, whether written or unwritten, or concerning Revelation; but there is the greatest possible consensus of opinion concerning the right conformation of the faculties. . . . If I am to make some survey of these faculties, in respect of a person's years and the degree of wisdom which it has pleased God to give him, I would say that children recognise and seek God in their own way in the form of happiness, and acknowledge Him in the spontaneous gratitude which they accord their benefactors. No trait, therefore, is so excellent as gratitude, nothing so base as ingratitude. And when gratitude is expressed by more mature persons and the Common Notions gradually reveal their objects more clearly, Religion becomes enriched and appears in a greater variety of ways, though no practice emerges which is more admirable than this gratitude. With the advantage of age, piety and holiness of life take deeper roots within the conscience, and give birth to a profound love and faith in God. . . . It may seem paradoxical that moral virtue which is so strict and severe is and always has been esteemed by men in every age and place and respected in every land, in spite of the fact that it conflicts with our physical and, I may say, agreeable feelings. But the reason for this is as follows. Since Nature unceasingly labours to deliver the soul from its physical burden, so Nature itself instils men with its secret conviction that virtue constitutes the most effective means by which our mind may be gradually separated and released from the body, and enter into its lawful realm. And though many arguments could be cited to the same purpose, I know no more convincing proof than the fact that it is only virtue that has the power to draw our soul from the delights which engulf it, and even to restore it to its native region, so that freed from the foul embrace of vice, and finally from the fear of death itself, it can apply itself to its proper function and attain inward everlasting joy.

The minds of men have always been filled with horror for their wickedness. Their vices and crimes have been obvious to them. They must be expiated by repentance.

There is no general agreement concerning the various rites or mysteries which the priests have devised for the expiation of sin. Among the Romans, ceremonies of purification, cleansing, atonement, among the Greeks, rites of expiation and purging, and in nearly all races, sacrifices, even of human victims, a cruel and abominable device of the priests, were instituted for this purpose. Among the Egyptians and all the heathen races observances of a similar kind prevailed. . . . Among the Mohammedans, Ramadan is held twice each year after the manner of our Forty Days. . . . General agreement among religions, the nature of divine goodness, and above all conscience, tell us that our crimes may be washed away by true penitence, and that we can be restored to new union with God. For this inner witness condemns wickedness while at the same time it can wipe out the stain of it by genuine repentance, as the inner form of apprehension under proper conditions proves. I do not wish to consider here whether any other more appropriate means exists by which the divine justice may be appeased, since I have undertaken in this work only to rely on truths which are not open to dispute but are derived from the evidence of immediate perception and admitted by the whole world. This alone I assert, whatever may be said to the contrary, that unless wickedness can be abolished by penitence and faith in God, and unless the Divine goodness can satisfy the Divine justice (and no further appeal can be invoked), then there does not exist, nor ever has existed any universal source to which the wretched mass of men, crushed beneath the burden of sin, can turn to obtain grace and inward peace. If this were the case, God has created and condemned certain men, in fact the larger part of the human race, not only without their desire, but without their knowledge. This idea is so dreadful and consorts so ill with the providence and goodness, and even the justice of God, that it is more charitable to suppose that the whole human race has always possessed in repentance the opportunity of becoming reconciled with God. And as long as men did not cut themselves off from it their damnation would not have been due to the benevolent will of God, but to their own sins, nor could God have been charged with blame if they failed to find salvation. All the teaching of the greatest preachers concerning eternal salvation coincides on this issue, since every means of redress is useless except penitence and becomes, as they tell us, empty and futile. Accordingly they hold it to be of such importance in relation to the divine goodness that they consider that when no readier way presents itself the entire secret of salvation may be revealed in this process. . . . To declare that God has cut us off from the means by which we can return to Him, provided that we play our part to the utmost of our ability, is a blasphemy so great that those who indulge in it seek to destroy not merely human goodness, but also the goodness of God. They must abandon these ideas, and their ideas and utterances, at least concerning the secret judgments of God, must be more guarded. For they cannot deny that if not from general providence, yet from particular providence or Grace, may flow the means by which God's favour may be won. . . . Now, if anyone with perverted curiosity asks me why we possess the liberty to commit sin and crime, I can only answer that it is due to the secret judgments of God. If he persists in asking what can be known within the moderate limits of the human faculties, I must reply that man is a finite animal, and therefore cannot do anything which is absolutely good or even absolutely bad. Yet the nature of each is modified in every action, so that the action shares to some extent in both, though it is named according to the element which has the larger share. . . .

There is Reward or Punishment after this life.

The rewards that are eternal have been variously placed in heaven, in the stars, in the Elysian fields, or in contemplation. Punishment has been thought to lie in metempsychosis, in hell (which some describe as filled with fire, but the Chinese imagine pervaded with smoke), or in some infernal regions, or regions of the middle air, or in temporary or everlasting death. But all religion, law, philosophy and, what is more, conscience, teach openly or implicitly that punishment or reward awaits us after this life. . . . In this sense there is no nation, however barbarous, which has not and will not recognise the existence of punishments and rewards. That reward and punishment exist is, then, a Common Notion, though there is the greatest difference of opinion as to their nature, quality, extent and mode. It is no objection that the soul perishes with the body, as some people assert. For they refer this very fact to punishment for sin, or else they mean only that part of the soul with which they have been familiar, namely, the physical senses; or finally they must be ignored since they talk sheer nonsense; for there is nothing in the faculties of the mind to suggest such ideas. That the soul could be immortal if God willed it is clearly a Common Notion in that among the most distant races, seething with every type of superstition, there exists a general conviction that purity of life and courage of mind promote happiness. It is on this account that they are said to honour the bones of those who have died bravely in battle. But I do not trouble myself about such matters, since I am not concerned with superstitions and sacred rites; it is not what a large number of men assert, but what all men of normal mind believe, that I find important. Scanning the vast array of absurd fictions I am content to discover a tiny Common Notion. And this is of the utmost importance, since when the general mass of men have rejected a whole range of beliefs which it has found valueless, it proceeds to acquire new beliefs by this method, until the point is reached where faith can be applied.

It follows from these considerations that the Dogmas which recognise a sovereign Deity, enjoin us to worship Him, command us to live a holy life, lead us to repent our sins, and warn us of future recompense or punishment, proceed from God and are inscribed within us in the form of Common Notions. But those dogmas which postulate a plurality of Gods, which do not forbid crimes and sins, which rail against penitence, and which express doubts about the eternal state of the soul, cannot be considered either Common Notions or truths. Accordingly every religion, if we consider it comprehensively, is not good; nor can we admit that salvation is open to men in every religion. For how could anyone who believes more than is necessary, but who does less than he ought, be saved? But I am convinced that in every religion, and indeed in every individual conscience, either through Grace or Nature, sufficient means are granted to men to win God's good will; while all additional and peculiar features which are found at any period must be referred to their inventors. It is not sufficient that they should be old if they have once been new. Ideas which are superfluous or even false may be not only novel but ancient, and truths which are only seized by a few cannot be essential to all. . . . I do not deny that sacred ceremonies can form part of religion; on the contrary I find that some ceremonies are included in every religion and serve to embellish it; so far they are valuable. But when they are made by the priests the essential elements of divine worship, then religion, and we who practise it are the victims of imposture. Rites must be kept within bounds. We can only accept them on the understanding that religion is chaste and only requires such ornaments as render a matron more venerable and respected. When she paints and dyes herself, her appearance is too suggestive of the harlot.

Such, then, are the Common Notions of which the true Catholic or universal church is built. For the church which is built of clay or stone or living rock or even of marble cannot be claimed to be the infallible Church. The true Catholic Church is not supported on the inextricable confusion or oral and written tradition to which men have given their allegiance. Still less is it that which fights beneath any one particular standard, or is comprised in one organisation so as to embrace only a restricted portion of the earth, or a single period of history. The only Catholic and uniform Church is the doctrine of Common Notions which comprehends all places and all men. This Church alone reveals Divine Universal Providence, or the wisdom of Nature. This Church alone explains why God is appealed to as the common Father. And it is only through this Church that salvation is possible. The adoration which has been bestowed on every particular Church belong to it. Every Church, as I have pointed out above, is the more exposed to error the further it is separated from it. Anyone who courts uncertain doctrines in place of the sure truths of divine providence, and forges new articles of Faith, forsakes this Church. If, however, anyone receives some truth by revelation, which I think can occur both in the waking state and in sleep, he must use it as occasion warrants, remembering that unless he is entrusted with a message of interest to all, he should reserve it to himself. For it is not likely that what is not evident to the faculties of all, can have any bearing on the whole human race. I have often observed that we can take much on faith with true piety, and we need not abandon any belief as long as it does not conflict with the divine attributes. It is not the case therefore, as some critic may point out, that after examining the means by which Divine Universal Providence acts and admitting that it is universal in its operation, I then restrict it to its own kingdom. I desire that every feature which redounds to the glory of God may be added to the characteristics which have been mentioned. For my part I accept with earnest faith and gratitude all that preceding ages have uttered in praise of God's goodness and mercy. I agree with the majority of mankind that all that they tell us not merely could have come to pass but that it actually did so. . . . This does not exclude the right of the church to decide matters which concern external worship, or ecclesiastical organization, or the publication for future generations of the records of earlier times, and especially those events which confirm the true attributes of God. . . . Whether indeed human wisdom has undertaken this examination in any age or place, or whether, even if it has done so, all who have rejected the inferior and trifling portions of religion, or possibly have accepted a mystical interpretation of them on the authority of their priests, equally enjoy the supreme happiness, I have not attempted to discuss. I firmly maintain, however, that it is and always has been possible for all men to reach the truths I have described. But whether they have been manifest, or whether, even when they are manifest they are immediately accepted, I am so far from wishing to discuss that all matters of this nature which depend upon the secret counsels of God, I leave to be inferred from the Divine wisdom and goodness. But if anyone calls them in dispute, I am prepared stoutly to defend them. For by no other method could the existence of Divine Universal Providence, the highest attribute of God, be proved by the principles of common reason. If we abandon these principles—and as I have often pointed out Nature or the Common Providence of the world does not operate beyond the means at its disposal— and if we give way to wicked blasphemies, terrible crimes, and finally to impenitence, to which we are sacramentally bound; if we defile the purity of Religion with foolish superstitions and degrading legends; it would be wholly unjust to blame the Supreme Goodness for our sins. It would be like accusing a host who provides a feast set out with a splendid profusion of dishes, of encouraging drunkenness, gluttony and license. For what is sufficient is due to God, excess is due to us. Why, then, as I have said elsewhere, following the law of common reason, can we not apply the same rule to the perfect sphere of the religion of God that we apply to any circle? If anything is added to it, or taken from it its shape is destroyed, and its perfection ruined. . . .

ON REVELATION

Revealed truth exists; and it would be unjust to ignore it. But its nature is quite distinct from the truth discussed above, in that the truth as I have defined it is based upon our faculties, while the truth of revelation depends upon the authority of him who reveals it. We must, then, proceed with great care in discerning what actually is revealed. Since there may be false revelations, I think it is hardly sufficient to apprehend what is revealed except through our faculties. But I believe that we can trust revelation when the following conditions occur. The first is that we must employ prayers, vows, faith and every faculty which can be used to invoke particular and general providence. The second is that revelation must be given directly to some person; for what is received from others as revelation must be accounted not revelation but tradition or history. And since the truth of history or of tradition depends upon him who recounts it, its foundations lie outside us, and in consequence it is, so far as we are concerned, mere possibility. The third condition is that revelation must recommend some course of action which is good; in this way genuine revelations may be distinguished from false and wicked temptations. The fourth condition is that the breath of the Divine Spirit must be immediately felt, for in this way we can distinguish the inner efforts of the faculties for truth from revelations which come from without us. When, therefore, what comes to us surpasses human understanding and all the preceding conditions are present, and we feel the Divine guidance in our activities, we must recognise with reverence the good will of God. We cannot indeed prescribe the way in which true revelation must be conveyed to us; it is beyond our power to formulate laws for events which are supernatural. We must, then, regard Revelation as divine, whether it comes during sleep or when we are awake, in ecstasy, in speaking, in reading, or in any other way, whenever the conditions which I have enumerated occur. But we must take great care to avoid deception, for men who are depressed, superstitious, or ignorant of causes are always liable to it. . . . As for the means of revelation it is generally held that revelations are most frequently made with the medium of spirits which have been recognized in all ages as a special order of beings, invisible, impalpable, free of physical substance, endowed with rapid movement, and variously called angels, demons, intelligences and geniuses. Some doubt, however, exists concerning their nature. Some people imagine them to be good, others think they are evil, so that we can reasonably leave their real character an open question. But this need not disturb us, as long as the preceding conditions are present, for otherwise no announcement of this kind can possibly come from God. But if we can only place confidence in revelation when it is given under the conditions which I have laid down, what are we to think of those revelations which are solemnly asserted by the priests to have occurred in former ages? Must we place greater faith in them? In spite of such a body of authority the ordinary layman may fairly demand from his priest the following criteria, in addition to those already enumerated. Firstly, that it be proved beyond all doubt that a revelation has been given to the priest. Secondly, that the revelation should have proceeded from the supreme God, speaking with His own voice, as He is said formerly to have done, or through the agency of some good angel. Thirdly, that the revelation of oracle or utterance should have been accurately expressed and reported by the priest; or when it had to be written down and transmitted to posterity through the priest's script. it should have been possible fully to correct and restore it in the light of this transcription, in case any addition, omission, or alteration had been made in the succeeding centuries. Fourthly, the revelation should concern later ages so closely that it necessarily becomes an article of Faith; particularly since nearly all such points depend upon confidence in a single witness. A priest should offer satisfactory credentials on all these points before the layman can yield implicit trust in his revelation. If the priest should fail in this, the cautious layman may not arrive at any conclusion by means of the alleged revelation which he could not have gathered apart from it; such as ideas of a better life, and similar notions which, as I have shown above, are written in our hearts. . . .

Though the layman plays his own part in this discussion, it will not be permissible for him to draw any conclusion contrary to those dogmas which have been fully sanctioned by the authority of the true Catholic Church, and published to the glory of the supreme God. If revelation is taken in a more general sense it includes whatever is required of God's grace. In this sense the succour sent from heaven to lost souls at times of affliction in response to their prayers is revelation. So, too, are those intimate divine apprehensions concerning faith, good works, and repentance. Movements of conscience and prayerful impulses have their beginning and end in revelation. In a word every original impulse of pity and joy which springs in our hearts is a revelation. More strictly, however, the only revelations are those which are recognized by the inner perception to lie beyond the scope of general providence. For this reason if we did not possess a supernatural and miraculous sense we should be obliged to hold that God confined Himself to His universal providence, and disclosed Himself only through those faculties of faith and prayer which are implanted in every normal human being. These considerations, therefore, serve to distinguish what is due to universal providence, what to special providence, and what are genuine revelations. . . . I do not hesitate to repeat that our actions are perfected and brought to completion only by Grace. Yet under the guidance of the inner consciousness I maintain that the principles of good actions spring from Common Notions, or the divine wisdom within us. Accordingly I think it is certain that no human being can so deafen his conscience as to lose his power of distinguishing, in any particular case, between good and evil. Thus when evil has been done owing to a failure to perceive the distinction, and the inward consciousness causes the sinner profound trouble of mind, and fills him with disgust; when he comes to repent his misdeeds so as to turn from them with horror, and bends all his endeavours to change his ways; when he directs himself with prayers and vows towards God, before Whom his conscience forthwith displays its guilt, and decides upon a better manner of life; in all this it is clear that nothing falls outside the sphere of common Grace. So far, then, the universal providence of God applies. But when in a moment of intense faith we make a special appeal to God, and feel within us His saving power and a sense of marvellous deliverance, I do not doubt that the mind is touched by Grace, or particular providence, and that since some new aspect of God is revealed, we pass beyond the normal level of experience. . . .

Now though I consider all the articles of faith shine by their own glory, so that unless they receive their authority from some personal revelation they are subject to examination in the same ways as other judgments; yet since there is no means which God in His great goodness may not employ, it is no less important to examine the instrument through which the revelation is transmitted than the nature of the mode of perception which is used. . . . Before I pass on to discuss probability I wish briefly to consider whether the precepts contained in the Decalogue are Common Notions or revealed truths. For my part I am certain that they ought to be counted Common Notions, since their injunctions are implicit in every kind of law and religion. I have often observed that the universal providence which governs empires does not fail to operate in matters of necessity. We cannot believe, then, that whatever the diverse sources of these commands are, and though many of them have come to be mixed with elements which have little relation to piety and justice, yet they cannot be thought without sacrilege to have been established apart from the Common Notions. It is of no importance whether sacred priests or legislators promulgated these laws, since the wisest men of antiquity taught that the observance of them was sanctioned not only by the Civil code but also by religion. They are therefore Common Notions. But since we may easily fall into error in the process of giving an account of them, it is reasonable to suppose that God Himself has granted us some indication of them in His mercy, and in a special Divine way. So, firstly, the highest respect is due to God, according to a Common Notion; and lest men should suppose that persons distinguished for holiness of life deserve some special form of worship, He commands that He only should be worshipped. Secondly, since men were able to form some image, which could arouse reverence and veneration, He forbade all kinds of symbols and images. Thirdly, since this supreme goodness may be treated lightly and with contempt, and so come to be slandered in frivolous deed or word, God does not allow us to use His name in vain. Fourthly, for fear that men should be destroyed by labour and toil, or on the other hand should enjoy too much leisure (for leisure is of God and is a Common Notion) He ordered that six days should be given to work and care, the seventh to rest and the worship of God. Fifthly, lest men might look upon their relation to their parents as a kind of first cause, and should therefore accord them divine worship, He has taught us what benefit we may hope for from honouring our parents. Sixthly, lest men should injure themselves or others except under the need of self-preservation, He has forbidden murder. Seventhly, lest men should suppose that in love anything may be permitted, He does not allow adultery. Eighthly, He has forbidden theft, lest men should seize another's property to increase their own goods. Ninthly, He prohibits false witness, so that truth may stand secure. And finally, lest men should think they can encroach on the rights of others, which they all hold according to their deserts, He enjoins on each contentedness of heart. These commandments, therefore, constitute a summary of Common Notions. But since it is easy to add to them, we must faithfully believe that God has given us forewarning of them by revelation or particular providence; and this I believe more readily since though our parents lived in earlier ages under conditions in which the law of Nature was inviolate, yet because in process of time their hearts became corrupt, it is reasonable to suppose that God prescribed the foregoing rules as guides to a better life.

A Summary Account of
the Deists' Religion*

Charles Blount

Herbert had relatively few followers. Though theological controversy went on, through civil war and Commonwealth, complacent Restoration and Glorious Revolution, though Calvinist sects argued with one another on church organization and with Anglicans on church appointments and on theological questions, deists remained rare. Everyone—or nearly everyone—professed belief in special revelation, in the divinity of Jesus Christ, and in the advantages of a national church. There were a few Socinians (that is to say, Unitarians), but they were for the most part obscure. And Hobbes, widely regarded as an atheist or, by some, as a deist, had a terrible reputation. It was not until the turbulent 1680s that Herbert found a true successor in Charles Blount (1654-1693).

Blount, indeed, followed Herbert closely; his seven essential articles of natural religion are simply restatements of Herbert's five common religious notions. His writings, marked by some vigor and a good deal of useful classical learning, have received relatively little attention; partly, at least, because his biographers have condescended to him for his committing suicide. "Poor Blount,"—the "poor" is significant—"sent a bullet through his brains in 1693, because the law would not permit him to marry his deceased wife's sister." [1] Thus Sir Leslie Stephen. But Blount, in addition to preaching what was to become staple deist preachment—the sufficiency of natural religion—did make one contribution to the deist debate: by utilizing his wide classical learning, Blount demonstrated how to use pagan writers, and pagan ideas,

---

* This excerpt from a short tract is taken from *The Miscellaneous Works of Charles Blount* (1695), 88-93.

[1] Leslie Stephen, *History of English Thought in the Eighteenth Century,* I, 194.

against Christianity. This had to some extent been done before: every educated Christian, after all, was a scholar of the pagan classics. But Blount—even in the brief excerpt printed below— confronted Christianity and paganism quite radically. Other deists were to follow his lead.

CHAP. I.

The Deists Opinion of God.

Whatsover is Adorable, Amiable, and Imitable by Mankind, is in one Supream infinite and perfect Being: *Satis est nobis Deus unus.*

CHAP. II.

Concerning the Manner of Worshipping God.

First, Negatively, it is not to be by an Image; for the first Being is not sensible, but intelligible: *Pinge sonum,* puts us upon an impossibility; no more can an infinite mind be represented in matter.

Secondly, Nor by Sacrifice; for *Sponsio non valet ut alter pro altero puniatur:* However, no such *Sponsio* can be made with a bruit Creature; nor if God loves himself, as he is the highest Good, can any External Rite, or Worship re-instate the Creature, after sin, in his favour, but only Repentance, and Obedience for the future, ending in an Assimulation to himself, as he is the highest Good: And this is the first Error in all particular Religions, that external things or bare Opinions of the Mind, can after sin propitiate God. Hereby particular Legislators have endeared themselves and flattered their Proselytes into good Opinions of them, and Mankind willingly submitted to the Cheat; *Enim facilius est superstitiose, quam juste vivere.*

Thirdly. Not by a Mediator; for, 1*st.* It is unnecessary, *Misericordia Dei* being *sufficiens Fustitiæ suæ.* 2*ly,* God must appoint this Mediator, and so was really reconciled to the World before. And 3*ly,* A Mediator derogates from the infinite mercy of God, equally as an Image doth from his *Spiritualitie* and *Infinitie.*

Secondly, Positively, by an inviolable adherence in our lives to all the things φυσει διχαια, by an imitation of God in all his imitable Perfections, especially his Goodness, and believing magnificiently of it.

CHAP. III.

Of Punishments after this Life.

A man that is endued with the same Vertues we have before mentioned, need not fear to trust his Soul with God after death: For first, no Creature could be made with a malevolent intent, the first Good who is also the first Principle of all Beings hath but one Affection or Property, and that is Love; which was long before there was any such thing as Sin. 2dly, At death he goes to God, one and the same being, who in his own nature for the Sins of the Penitent hath as well an inclination to Pity as Justice, and there is nothing dreadful in the whole Nature of God, but his Justice, no Attribute else being terrible. 3dly, Infinite Power is ever safe and need not revenge for self-preservation. 4thly, However *Verisimile est, similem Deo a Deo non negligi.*

CHAP. IV.

The Probability of such a Deist's Salvation before the credulous and ill-living Papists.

1. To be sure he is no Idolator. The *Jew* and the *Mahometan* accuse the Christians of Idolatry, the Reform'd Churches, the *Roman,* the *Socinian* the other Reformed Churches, the *Deists* the *Socinian* for his *Deus factus;* but none can accuse the *Deist* of Idolatry, for he only acknowledges one Supream Everlasting God, and thinks magnificently of him.

2dly, The Morality in Religion is above the Mystery in it; for, 1. The Universal sense of Mankind in the Friendships Men make, sheweth this; for who does not value good Nature, Sincerity and Fidelity in a Friend, before subtilty of Understanding; & *Religio & quædam, cum Deo amicitia:* An unity of nature and will with God, that is the Root of the Dearest Friendships. Then, 2dly, it is an everlasting Rule that runs through all Beings, *Simile a simili amatur,* God cannot love what is unlike him. Now, 3dly, here lies our trial, here is the scene of our obedience, and here are our conflicts with our Passions; if this be true, then the credulous Christian that believes Orthodoxly, but lives ill, is not safe.

3*dly,* If the *Deist* errs, he errs not like a fool, but *secundum Verbum,* after enquiry, and if he be sincere in his Principles, he can when dying appeal to God, *Te, bone Deus, quæsivi per omnia.* . . .

1. The Grand *Arcanum* of Religion among the *Pythagoreans* was that the Object of Divine Worship is one, and invisible; *Plutarch* cites this in the Life of *Numa,* as the Dogma of *Pythagoras,* and accordingly his Followers used no Images in their Worships.

2. The Heathens, notwithstanding their particular and Topical Deities, acknowledged one supream God, not *Jupiter* of *Crete,* but the Father of Gods and Men: Only they said this Supream God being of so high a nature, and there being other intermediate Beings betwixt God and Mankind, they were to address themselves to them as Mediators to carry up their Prayers, and bring down his Blessings; so as the Opinion of the necessity of a Mediator was the foundation of the Heathen Idolatry, they could not go to the Fountain of Good it self. The Popist Religion stands on the same foundation; whereas the greatest Goodness is the most accessible; which shews that Popery was a Religion accommodated to the Sentiments of Mankind from precedent Religions, and not to infallible Reason drawn from the eternal respects of things. And Reason being the first relation of God, is first to be believed, not depending on doubtful fact without us, but full of its own light shining always in us.

3*dly,* It was the common sense of the wisest Philosophers, that things were good antecedent to all humane Compacts; and this Opinion. *Pyrrho* in *Sextus Empericus* argues against: Also Mr. *Hobbs* hath of late revived in the World *Pyrrho*'s Doctrin, tho' without reason; for as there are immediate Propositions, to which the understanding (*sine discursu*) assents, as soon as proposed, so are there things good and just which they will at first view, without deliberation, approve of and chose also, (*viz.*) the Veneration of an Almighty invisible Being, referring of our selves to him, with a (*siat voluntas tua*) abhorrence of breach of contract with man, of a lye, as a violation of Truth; so as in my judgment, there is a sanction arising from the nature of things, before any Law declared amongst men: That there is a *genero-sum honestum* hid in all our Souls is plain from the *Epicurean* Deists themselves, for they labour to have their Vices imputed rather to a Superiority of their reason above that of others, than to a servitude of their reason to their own passions; which shews Vice is naturally esteemed a base and low thing. This appears from the Legislators of the World, as *Numa, Zamolxis,* &c. . . .

B. ENGLISH DEISM, THE MAJOR WRITERS

READING NO. 3

Christianity not Mysterious*

John Toland

The deist debate got under way in really dramatic fashion in the middle of the 1690s. John Locke published his The Reasonableness of Christianity *in 1695; John Toland published his* Christianity not Mysterious *in 1696. The two titles are similar, but, as Sir Leslie Stephen has rightly pointed out, they enshrine a fundamental, and fundamentally irreconcilable, disagreement: "Locke had argued that Christianity was reasonable. Toland added that there was no nonsense in Christianity. What was the difference between the two propositions? In the opinion of his antagonists, the main difference was that the very title of the book involves a subterfuge. Christianity must be taken to mean —not the historical creed of Christendom—but pure and undefiled religion; and as the accepted creed undeniably includes mysterious doctrines, his argument amounted to the assertion that the creed was so far false." [1] This, of course, was the single step Locke had not wanted to take. Locke wanted to rescue Christianity; Toland, his professions to the contrary, wanted to subvert it. To say that Christianity is reasonable, and that, to the extent that it is not reasonable, it is not Christianity, is to redefine Christianity as a purely natural religion and thus make Christianity, which after all has some unique characteristics, unnecessary. As a twentieth-century theologian like Tillich might say: complete demythologization of Christianity is impossible; the moment it succeeds, Christianity is dead or, at least, redundant.*

* The following selection is taken from John Toland, *Christianity not Mysterious: or, a Treatise Shewing that There is Nothing in the Gospel Contrary to Reason, Nor Above It* (1696), pp. 23-61, 68-74, 158-173.

[1] Sir Leslie Stephen, *History of English Thought in the Eighteenth Century*, I, 105.

There is some irony in this situation. John Toland was John Locke's declared but unwelcome disciple; in his theory of knowledge, Toland followed Locke's sensationalism, and followed it intelligently. His main line of attack—the attack on mysteries— was Lockian through and through. And in the time that he published his most important work, he loudly, if perhaps not wholly sincerely, proclaimed himself a Christian and a loyal subject of the Church of England. But in making Locke's compromise with revelation impossible—in arguing that whatever was unreasonable could not be credible or admirable—Toland certainly went beyond Locke's spirit and intentions.

Toland paid for his audacity. He began life as a Roman Catholic, and then moved to Latitudinarianism, deism, and finally pantheism, but in consequence he found it hard to make a respectable career. At times he found it safer to live abroad. But he was an interesting man with an inquiring mind. Christianity not Mysterious, *though not his first publication, is his first serious, and remains his best book. His life of Milton, which came out in 1697, and* Amyntor *(1698), raised deistic doubts about the authenticity of the canon of Scriptures. In his* Letters to Serena *(1704), addressed to the Prussian queen, Toland speculated upon the natural, psychological origins of religious beliefs; in his* Nazarenus *(1718), he returned to his case made in* Christianity not Mysterious: *whatever goes beyond natural religion in Christian worship is unworthy of true religion and a priestly interpolation. Finally, in his* Pantheisticon, *published in 1720, two years before his death, Toland gave sympathetic treatment to Spinoza's pantheism without wholly, or openly, committing himself to it. The experimental quality of his mind, and its naturalistic temper, stamp Toland as an eighteenth-century man. The distance from such seventeenth-century deists as Herbert, as I have said before, is marked.*

SECT. II.

That the Doctrines of the Gospel are not contrary to Reason.

[W]hat is evidently repugnant to clear and distinct Idea's, or to our common Notions, is contrary to Reason: I go on therefore

to prove, that *the Doctrines of the Gospel,* if it be the Word of God, *cannot be so.* But if it be objected, that very few maintain they are: I reply, that no *Christian* I know of now (for we shall not disturb the Ashes of the Dead) expresly says *Reason* and the *Gospel* are contrary to one another. But, which returns to the same, very many affirm, that though the Doctrines of the latter cannot in themselves be contradictory to the Principles of the former, as proceeding both from God; yet, that according to our Conceptions of them, *they may seem directly to clash:* And that though we cannot reconcile them by reason of our corrupt and limited Understandings; yet that from the Authority of *Divine Revelation,* we are bound to believe and acquiesce in them; or, as the *Fathers* taught 'em to speak, *to adore what we cannot comprehend.*

CHAP. I.

The Absurdity and Effects of admitting any real or seeming Contradictions in Religion.

This famous and admirable Doctrine is the undoubted Source of all the *Absurdities* that ever were seriously vented among *Christians.* Without the Pretence of it, we should never hear of the *Transubstantiation,* and other ridiculous Fables of the Church of *Rome;* nor of any of the *Eastern Ordures,* almost all receiv'd into this *Western Sink:* Nor should we be ever banter'd with the *Lutheran Impanation,* or the *Ubiquity* it has produc'd, as one Monster ordinarily begets another. And tho the *Socinians* disown this Practice, I am mistaken if either they or the *Arians* can make their Notions of a *dignifi'd and Creature-God capable of Divine Worship,* appear more reasonable than the Extravagancies of other Sects touching the Article of the *Trinity.*

In short, this Doctrine is the known Refuge of some Men, when they are at a loss in explaining any Passage of the Word of God. Lest they should appear to others less knowing than they would be thought, they make nothing of fathering that upon the secret Counsels of the Almighty, or the Nature of the Thing, which is indeed the Effect of Inaccurate Reasoning, Unskilfulness in the Tongues, or Ignorance of History. But more commonly it is the Consequence of *early Impressions,* which they dare seldom afterwards correct by more free and riper Thoughts: So *desiring to be Teachers of the Law, and understanding neither what they say, nor those things which they affirm* [1 Tim. 1. 7], they obtrude upon us *for Doctrines the Commandments of Men* [Mat. 15. 9]. And truly well they may; for if we once admit this Principle, I know not what we can deny that is told us in the Name of the Lord. This Doctrine, I must remark it too, does highly concern us of the *Laity;* for however it came to be first establish'd, the *Clerg*y (always excepting such as deserve it) have not been since wanting to themselves, but improv'd it so far as not only to make the plainest, but the most trifling things in the World *mysterious,* that we might constantly depend upon them for the Explication. And, nevertheless they must not, if they could, explain them to us without ruining their own Design, let them never so fairly pretend it. But, overlooking all Observations proper for this Place, let us enter upon the immediate Examen of the Opinion it self.

The first thing I shall insist upon is, that if any Doctrine of the *New Testament* be contrary to Reason, we have no manner of Idea of it. To say, for instance, that *a Ball is white and black at once,* is to say just nothing; for these Colours are so incompatible in the same Subject, as to exclude all Possibility of a real positive Idea or Conception. So to say, as the *Papists,* that *Children dying before Baptism are damn'd without Pain,* signifies nothing at all: For if they be intelligent Creatures in the other World, to be eternally excluded God's Presence, and the Society of the Blessed, must prove ineffable Torment to them: But if they think they have no Understanding, then they are not capable of Damnation in their Sense; and so they should not say they are in *Limbo*-Dungeon; but that either they had no Souls, or were annihilated; which (had it been true, as they can never shew) would be reasonable enough, and easily conceiv'd. Now if we have no Idea's of a thing, it is certainly but lost Labour for us to trouble our selves about it: For what I don't conceive, can no more give me right Notions of God, or influence my Actions, than a Prayer deliver'd in an unknown Tongue can excite my Devotion: *If the Trumpet gives an uncertain Sound, who shall prepare himself to the Battel? And except Words easy to be understood be utter'd, how shall it be known what is spoken?*

[1 Cor. 14. 8, 9] Syllables, though never so well put together, if they have not Idea's fix'd to them, are but *Words spoken in the Air* [Ver. 9]; and cannot be the Ground of a *reasonable Service* [Rom. 12. 1], or Worship.

If any should think to evade the Difficulty by saying, that the Idea's of certain Doctrines may be contrary indeed to common Notions, yet consistent with themselves, and I know not what supra-intellectual Truths, he's but just where he was. But supposing a little that the thing were so; it still follows, that none can understand these Doctrines except their Perceptions be communicated to him in an extraordinary manner, as by new Powers and Organs. And then too, others cannot be edifi'd by what is discours'd of 'em, unless they enjoy the same Favour. So that if I would go preach the Gospel to the *Wild Indians,* I must expect the Idea's of my Words should be, I know not how, infus'd into their Souls in order to apprehend me: And according to this Hypothesis, they could no more, without a Miracle, understand my Speech than the chirping of Birds; and *if they knew not the Meaning of my Voice, I should* even *to them be a Barbarian* [1 Cor. 14. 11], nowithstanding *I spoke Mysteries in the Spirit* [Ver. 2]. But what do they mean by consisting with themselves, yet not with our common Notions? *Four* may be call'd *Five* in Heaven; but so the Name only is chang'd, the Thing remains still the same. And since we cannot in this World know any thing but by our common Notions, how shall we be sure of this pretended Consistency between our present seeming Contradictions, and the Theology of the World to come? For as 'tis by *Reason* we arrive at the Certainty of God's own Existence, so we cannot otherwise discern his *Revelations* but by their Conformity with our natural Notices of him, which is in so many words, to agree with our common Notions.

The next thing I shall remark is, That those, who stick not to say *they could believe a downright Contradiction to Reason, did they find it contain'd in the Scripture,* do justify all Absurdities whatsoever; and by opposing one Light to another, undeniably make God the Author of all Incertitude. The very Supposition, that Reason might authorize one thing, and the Spirit of God another, throws us into inevitable *Scepticism;* for we shall be at a perpetual Uncertainty which to obey: Nay, we can never be sure which is which. For the Proof of the Divinity of *Scripture* depending upon Reason, if the clear Light of the one might be any way contradicted, how shall we be convinc'd of the Infallibility of the other? Reason may err in this Point as well as in any thing else; and we have no particular Promise it shall not, no more than the *Papists* that their Senses may not deceive them in every thing as well as in *Transubstantiation*. To say it bears witness to it self, is equally to establish the *Alcoran* or the *Poran*. And 'twere a notable Argument to tell a *Heathen*, that the *Church* has declared it, when all Societies will say as much for themselves, if we take their word for it. Besides, it may be, he would ask whence the *Church* had Authority to decide this Matter? And if it should be answer'd from the *Scripture*, a thousand to one but he would divert himself with this Circle. You must believe that the *Scripture* is Divine, because the *Church* has so determined it, and the *Church* has this deciding Authority from the *Scripture*. 'Tis doubted if this Power of the *Church* can be prov'd from the Passages alledged to that Purpose; but the *Church* it self (a Party concern'd) affirms it. Hey-day! are not these eternal Rounds very exquisite Inventions to giddy and entangle the Unthinking and the Weak?

But if we believe the *Scripture* to be Divine, not upon its own bare Assertion, but from a real Testimony consisting in the Evidence of the things contain'd therein; from undoubted Effects, and not from Words and Letters; what is this but to prove it by *Reason?* It has in it self, I grant, the brightest Characters of *Divinity:* But 'tis *Reason* finds them out, examines them, and by its Principles approves and pronounces them sufficient; which orderly begets in us an Acquiescence of *Faith* or Perswasion. Now if Particulars be thus severely sifted; if not only the Doctrine of *Christ* and his *Apostles* be consider'd, but also their Lives, Predictions, Miracles, and Deaths; surely all this Labour would be in vain, might we upon any account dispense with Contradictions. O! blessed and commodious System, that dischargest at one stroak those troublesome Remarks about History, Language, figurative and literal Senses, Scope of the Writer, Circumstances, and other Helps of Interpretation! We judg of a Man's Wisdom and Learning by his Actions, and his Discourses; but God, who we are assur'd *has not left himself without a Witness* [Acts 14.

17], must have no Privileges above the maddest Enthusiast, or the *Devil* himself, at this rate.

But a Veneration for the very Words of God will be pretended: This we are pleas'd with; for we know *that God is not a Man that he should lie* [Num. 23. 19]. But the Question is not about the Words, but their Sense, which must be always worthy of their Author, and therefore according to the Genius of all Speech, figuratively interpreted, when occasion requires it. Otherwise, under pretence of *Faith in the Word of God,* the highest Follies and Blasphemies may be deduc'd from the Letter of *Scripture;* as, that God is subject to Passions, is the Author of Sin, that *Christ* is a Rock, was actually guilty of and defil'd with our Transgressions, that we are Worms or Sheep, and no Men. And if a Figure be admitted in these Passages, why not, I pray, in all Expressions of the like Nature, when there appears an equal Necessity for it?

It may be demanded why I have so long insisted upon this Article, since that none expresly makes *Scripture* and *Reason* contradictory, was acknowledg'd before. But in the same place mention is made of some who hold, *that they may seem directly to clash;* and that though we cannot reconcile them together, yet that we are bound to acquiesce in the Decisions of the former. A seeming Contradiction is to us as good as a real one; and our Respect for the *Scripture* does not require us to grant any such in it, but rather to conclude, that we are ignorant of the right Meaning when a Difficulty occurs; and so to suspend our Judgments concerning it, till with suitable Helps and Industry we discover the Truth. As for acquiescing in what a Man understands not, or cannot reconcile to his Reason, they know best the fruits of it that practise it. For my part, I'm a Stranger to it, and cannot reconcile my self to such a Principle. On the contrary, I am pretty sure he pretends in vain to convince the Judgment, who explains not the Nature of the Thing. A Man may give his verbal Assent to he knows not what, out of Fear, Superstition, Indifference, Interest, and the like feeble and unfair Motives: but as long as he conceives not what he believes, he cannot sincerely acquiesce in it, and remains depriv'd of all solid Satisfaction. He is constantly perplex'd with Scruples not to be remov'd by his *implicite Faith;* and so is ready to be shaken, and *carried away with every wind of Doctrine.* I will believe because I will believe, that is, *because I'm in the Humour so to do* [Ephes. 4. 14], is the top of his Apology. Such are unreasonable Men, *walking after the Vanity of their Minds, having their Understandings darkned, being Strangers to the Life of God through the Ignorance that is in them, because of the Hardness of their Hearts* [Ephes. 4. 7, 18]. But he that comprehends a thing, is as sure of it as if he were himself the Author. He can never be brought to suspect his Profession; and, if he be honest, will always render a pertinent account of it to others.

The natural Result of what has been said is, That to believe the Divinity of *Scripture,* or the Sense of any Passage thereof, without rational Proofs, and an evident Consistency, is a blameable Credulity, and a temerarious Opinion, ordinarily grounded upon an ignorant and wilful Disposition; but more generally maintain'd out of a gainful Prospect. For we frequently embrace certain Doctrines not from any convincing Evidence in them, but because they serve our Designs better than the Truth; and because other Contradictions we are not willing to quit, are better defended by their means.

CHAP. II.

Of the Authority of Revelation, *as it regards this Controversy.*

Against all that we have been establishing in this Section, *the Authority of Revelation* will be alledg'd with great shew, as if without a Right of silencing or extinguishing *Reason,* it were altogether useless and impertinent. But if the Distinction I made in the precedent Section, No 9. be well consider'd, the Weakness of the present Objection will quickly appear, and this Controversy be better understood hereafter. There I said *Revelation* was not a necessitating Motive of Assent, but *a Mean of Information.* We should not confound the Way whereby we come to the Knowledg of a thing, with the Grounds we have to believe it. A Man may inform me concerning a thousand Matters I never heard of before, and of which I should not as much as think if I were not told; yet I believe nothing purely upon his word without *Evidence* in the things themselves. Not the bare Authority of him that speaks, but the clear Conception I form of what he says, is the *Ground of my Perswasion.*

If the sincerest Person on Earth should assure me he saw a Cane without two ends, I neither should nor could believe him; because this Relation plainly contradicts the Idea of a Cane. But if he told me he saw a Staff that, being by chance laid in the Earth, did after sometime put forth Sprigs and Branches, I could easily rely upon his Veracity; because this no way contradicts the Idea of a Staff, nor transcends Possibility.

I say *Possibility;* for *Omnipotency* it self can do no more. They impose upon themselves and others, who require Assent to things contradictory, because *God,* say they, *can do all things, and it were limiting of his Power to affirm the contrary.* Very good! we heartily believe God can do all things: But that meer *Nothing* should be the Object of his Power, the very *Omnipotency* alledg'd, will not permit us to conceive. And that every *Contradiction,* which is a Synonym for *Impossibility,* is *pure nothing,* we have already sufficiently demonstrated. To say, for example, that *a thing is extended and not extended, is round and square at once,* is to say *nothing;* for these Idea's destroy one another, and cannot subsist together in the same Subject. But when we clearly perceive a perfect Agreement and Connection between the Terms of any Proposition, we then conclude it possible because intelligible: So I understand God may render immediately solid, what has been hitherto fluid; make present Beings cease to exist; and *call those things that are not, as tho they were* [Rom. 4. 17]. When we say then, *that nothing is impossible with God,* or that he can do all things, we mean whatever is possible in it self, however far above the Power of Creatures to effect.

Now, such is the Nature of a Matter of Fact, that though it may be conceiv'd possible enough, yet he only can with Assurance assert its Existence who is himself the Author, or by some *Means of Information* comes first to the certain Knowledg of it. That there was such an Island as *Jamaica,* no *European* could ever reasonably deny: And yet that it was precisely situated in such a Latitude, was water'd with those Rivers, cloth'd with these Woods, bore this Grain, produc'd that Plant, no *English-man* before the Discovery of *America,* could positively affirm.

Thus God is pleas'd to reveal to us in *Scripture* several wonderful Matters of Fact, as *the Creation of the World, the last Judgment,* and many other important Truths, which no Man left to himself could ever imagine, no more than any of my fellow-Creatures can be sure of my private Thoughts: *For who knoweth the things of a Man save the Spirit of a Man that is in him? even so the things of God knoweth none but the Spirit of God* [1 Cor. 2. 11]. But as *secret things belong unto the Lord;* so *those things which are reveal'd, belong unto us and to our Children* [Deut. 29. 29]. Yet, as we discours'd before, we do not receive them only because they are reveal'd: For besides the infallible Testimony of the Revelation from all requisite Circumstances, we must see in its Subject the indisputable Characters of *Divine Wisdom* and *Sound Reason;* which are the only Marks we have to distinguish the Oracles and Will of God, from the Impostures and Traditions of Men.

Whoever reveals any thing, that is, whoever tells us something we did not know before, *his Words must be intelligible, and the Matter possible.* This Rule holds good, let *God* or *Man* be the Revealer. If we count that Person a Fool who requires our Assent to what is manifestly incredible, how dare we blasphemously attribute to *the most perfect Being,* what is an acknowledg'd Defect in one of our selves? As for unintelligible Relations, we can no more believe them from the Revelation of God, than from that of Man; for the conceiv'd Idea's of things are the only Subjects of Believing, Denying, Approving, and every other Act of the Understanding: Therefore all Matters reveal'd by God or Man, must be *equally intelligible and possible;* so far both Revelations agree. But in this they differ, that though the Revelation of Man should be thus qualifi'd, yet *he may impose upon me as to the Truth of the thing:* whereas what God is pleas'd to discover to me is not only clear to my Reason, (without which his Revelation could make me no wiser) but likewise *it is always true.* A Man, for example, acquaints me that he has found a Treasure: This is plain and possible, but he may easily deceive me. God assures me, that he has form'd Man of Earth: This is not only possible to God, and to me very intelligible; but the thing is also most certain, *God not being capable to deceive me, as Man is.* We are then to expect the same degree of *Perspicuity* from God as from Man, tho' more of *Certitude* from the first than the last.

This Reason perswades, and the Scriptures expresly speak it. Those *Prophets* or *Dreamers* [Deut. 13. 1, 2, 3] were to be ston'd to Death that should go about to seduce the People from the Worship of One God to *Polytheism,* though they should confirm their Doctrine *by Signs and Wonders.* And *though a Prophet spoke in the Name of the Lord, yet if the thing prophesied did not come to pass,* it was to be a rational Sign *he spoke presumptuously of himself, and not of God* [Deut. 18. 21, 22]. It was reveal'd to the Prophet *Jeremy* in Prison, that his Uncle's Son would sell his Field to him, *but he did not conclude it to be the Word of the Lord till his Kinsman actually came to strike the Bargain with him* [Jer. 32. 7, 8]. The Virgin *Mary,* tho of that Sex that's least Proof against Flattery and Superstition, did not implicitely believe *she should bear a Child that was to be called the Son of the most High, and of whose Kingdom there should be no end* [Luke. 1. 34, 35], till the *Angel* gave her a satisfactory Answer to the strongest Objection that could be made: Nor did she then conclude (so unlike was she to her present Worshippers) it should unavoidably come to pass; but humbly acknowledging the Possibility [Ver. 38], and her own Unworthiness, she quietly wish'd and expected the event.

In how many places are we exhorted *to beware of false Prophets* and *Teachers, Seducers* and *Deceivers?* [Mat. 7. 14] [2 Tim. 3. 13] [Tit. 1. 10]. We are not only *to prove or try all things,* and *to hold fast that which is best* [1 Thess. 5. 21], but also *to try the Spirits whether they be of God* [1 Joh. 4. 1]. But how shall we try? how shall we discern? Not *as the Horse and Mule which have no Understanding* [Psal. 32. 9], but *as circumspect and wise Men* [Eph. 5. 15], *judging what is said* [1 Cor. 10. 15]. In a word, it was from clear and weighty Reasons, both as to Fact and Matter, and not by a blind Obedience, that the Men of God of old embrac'd his Revelations, which upon the like Account we receive of their hands. I am not ignorant how some boast they are strongly perswaded *by the illuminating and efficacious Operation of the Holy Spirit,* and that they neither have nor approve other Reasons of their *Faith:* But we shall endeavour in its proper place to undeceive them; for no Adversary, how absurd or trifling soever, ought to be superciliously disregarded by an unfeigned Lover of Men and Truth. So far of Revelation; only in making it a *Mean of Information,* I follow *Paul* himself, who tells the *Corinthians,* that *he cannot profit them except he speaks to them by Revelation, or by Knowledg, or by Prophesying, or by Doctrine* [1 Cor. 14. 6].

CHAP. III.

That by Christianity was intended a Rational and Intelligible Religion; prov'd from the Miracles, Method, and Stile of the New Testament.

What we discours'd of *Reason* before, and *Revelation* now, being duly weigh'd, all the Doctrines and Precepts of the New Testament (if it be indeed Divine) must consequently agree with *Natural Reason,* and our own ordinary Idea's. This every considerate and well-dispos'd Person will find by the careful Perusal of it: And whoever undertakes this Task, will confess the Gospel *not to be hidden from us, nor afar off, but very nigh us, in our Mouths, and in our Hearts* [Deut. 30. 11, 14]. It affords the most illustrious Examples of close and perspicuous Ratiocination conceivable; which is incumbent on me in the Explication of its *Mysteries,* to demonstrate. And tho the Evidence of *Christ's* Doctrine might claim the Approbation of the *Gentiles,* and its Conformity with the Types and Prophecies of the *Old Testament,* with all the Marks of the *Messiah* concurring in his Person, might justly challenge the Assent of his Countrymen; yet to leave no room for doubt, he proves his Authority and Gospel by such Works and Miracles as the stiff-necked *Jews* themselves could not deny to be Divine. *Nicodemus* says to him, *No Man can do these Miracles which thou dost, except God be with him* [Joh. 3. 2]. Some of the Pharisees acknowledg'd *no Sinner could do such things* [Joh. 9. 16]. And others, *that they exceeded the Power of the Devils* [Joh. 10. 21].

Jesus himself appeals to his very Enemies, ready to stone him for pretended Blasphemy, saying; *If I do not the Works of my Father, believe me not: But if I do, believe not me, believe the Works; that you may know, and believe that the Father is in me, and I in him* [Joh. 10. 37, 38]: That is, believe not rashly on me, and so give a Testimony to my Works; but search the *Scriptures,* which testify of the *Messiah;* consider the Works I do, whether they be such as become God, and are attributed to him: If they be, then conclude and believe that I am he, &c. In effect, several of the People said, *that Christ when he should come could do no greater Wonders* [Joh. 7. 31]; and *many of the Jews believ'd when they saw the Miracles which he did* [Joh. 2. 23].

How shall we escape, says the Apostle, *if we neglect so great a Salvation which at the first began to be spoken by the Lord, and was confirm'd unto us by them that heard him; God also bearing them witness with divers Miracles, and Gifts of the Holy Spirit, according to his own Will?* [Heb. 2. 3, 4] Those who heard *Christ,* the Author of our Religion, speak, and saw the Wonders which he wrought, *renounce all the hidden things of Dishonesty, all Craftiness and deceitful handling of the Word of God:* And *that they manifest nothing but Truth they commend themselves to every Man's Conscience* [2 Cor. 4. 2], that is, they appeal to every Man's Reason, *in the Sight of God. Peter* exhorts Christians *to be ready always to give an Answer to every one that asks them a Reason of their Hope* [1 Pet. 3. 15]. Now to what Purpose serv'd all these Miracles, all these Appeals, if no Regard was to be had of Mens Understandings? if the Doctrines of Christ were incomprehensible? or were we oblig'd to believe reveal'd Nonsense?

But to insist no longer upon such Passages, all Men will own the Verity I defend if they read the sacred Writings with that Equity and Attention that is due to meer Humane Works: Nor is there any different Rule to be follow'd in the Interpretation of *Scripture* from what is common to all other Books. Whatever unprejudic'd Person shall use those Means, will find them notorious Deceivers, or much deceiv'd themselves, who maintain the *New Testament* is written without any Order or certain Scope, but just as Matters came into the *Apostles* Heads, whether transported with Enthusiastick Fits, (as some will have it) or, according to others, for lack of good Sense and a liberal Education. I think I may justly say, that they are Strangers to true Method, who complain of this Confusion and Disorder. But the Proof of the Case depends not upon Generalities.

The Facility of the *Gospel* is not confin'd only to Method; for the Stile is also most easy, most natural, and in the common Dialect of those to whom it was immediately consign'd. Should any preach in *Xenophon*'s strain to the present *Greeks,* or in correct *English* to the Country-People in *Scotland,* 'twould cost them much more Time and Pains to learn the very Words, than the Knowledg of the things denoted by them. Of old, as well as in our time, the *Jews* understood *Hebrew* worse than the Tongues of those Regions where they dwelt. No Pretences therefore can be drawn from the Obscurity of the Language in favour of the *irrational Hypothesis:* for all Men are supposed to understand the daily Use of their Mother-Tongue; whereas the Stile of the Learned is unintelligible to the Vulgar. And the plainest Authors that write as they speak, without the Disguise of pompous Elegance, have ever been accounted the best by all good Judges. It is a visible Effect of Providence that we have in our Hands the Monuments of the *Old Testament,* which in the *New* are always suppos'd, quoted, or alluded to. Nor is that all, for the *Jewish* Service and Customs continue to this day. If this had been true of the *Greeks* and *Romans,* we should be furnish'd with those Helps to understand aright many unknown Particulars of their Religion, which makes us Rulers and Teachers in *Israel.* Besides, we have the *Talmud,* and other Works of the *Rabbins,* which, however otherwise useless, give us no small Light into the antient Rites and Language. And if after all we should be at a loss about the Meaning of any Expression, we ought rather to charge it upon Distance of Time, and the want of more Books in the same Tongue, than to attribute it to the Nature of the thing, or the Ignorance of the Author, who might be easily understood by his Country-men and Contemporaries. But no Truth is to be establish'd, nor Falshood confuted from such Passages, no more than any can certainly divine his Fortune from the Sound of *Bow-bell.*

If any object, that the *Gospel* is penn'd with little or no Ornament, that there are no choice of Words, nor studied Expressions in it; the Accusation is true, and the Apostles themselves acknowledg it: nor is there a more palpable Demonstration of their having design'd to be understood by all. *I came not to you,* says *Paul, with Excellency of Speech, or Wisdom, declaring unto you the Testimony of God. My Speech and my Preaching was not with enticing Words of humane Wisdom, but in Demonstration* [1 Cor. 2. 1], or Conviction *of the Spirit* [Ver. 4] or Mind, *and in Power* or Efficacy. This he speaks in reference to the *Philosophers* and *Orators* of those Times, whose Elocution, 'tis confess'd, was curious, and Periods elaborate, apt to excite the Admiration of the Hearers, but not to satisfy their Reasons; charming indeed their Senses whilest in the *Theatre*, or the *Temple*, but making them neither the better at home, nor the wiser abroad.

These Men, as well as many of their *modern Successors*, were fond enough of their own ridiculous Systems, *to count the things of God Foolishness* [1 Cor. 2. 14], because they did not agree with their precarious and sensual Notions; because every Sentence was not wrapp'd up in *Mystery*, and garnish'd with a Figure: not considering that only false or trivial Matters need the Assistance of alluring Harangues to perplex or amuse. But they were Enemies and Strangers to the Simplicity of Truth. All their Study, as we took notice, lay in tickling the Passions of the People at their Pleasure with bombast Eloquence and apish Gesticulations. They boasted their Talent of perswading for or against any thing. And as he was esteemed the best *Orator* that made the worst Cause appear the most equitable before the Judges, so he was the best *Philosopher* that could get the wildest Paradox to pass for Demonstration. They were only concern'd about their own Glory and Gain, which they could not otherwise support, but (according to an Artifice that never fails, and therefore ever practis'd) by imposing upon the People with their *Authority* and *Sophistry*, and *under pretence of instructing, dexterously detaining them in the grossest Ignorance.*

But the Scope of the *Apostles* was very different: Piety towards God, and the Peace of Mankind, was their Gain, and *Christ* and his *Gospel* their Glory. They came not magnifying nor exalting themselves, not imposing but declaring their Doctrine. They did not confound and mislead, but convince the Mind. They were employ'd to dispel Ignorance, to eradicate Superstition, to propagate Truth and Reformation of Manners; *to preach Deliverance to Captives* [Luk. 4. 18], (*i.e.*) the Enjoyment of Christian Liberty to the Slaves of the Levitical and Pagan Priesthoods, and to declare Salvation to repenting Sinners.

I shall add here some of the Characters which *David* gives

of the Law and Word of God, that we may admit nothing as the Will of Heaven but what is agreeable to them: *The Law of the Lord*, says he, *is perfect, converting the Soul. The Testimony of the Lord is sure, making wise the Simple. The Statutes of the Lord are right, rejoicing the Heart. The Commandment of the Lord is pure, enlightning the Eyes. The Fear of the Lord is clean, enduring for ever. The Judgments of the Lord are true and righteous altogether. I have more Understanding than all my Teachers, for thy Testimonies are my Meditation. I understand more than the Antients, because I kep thy Precepts. Thy Word is a Lamp unto my Feet, and a Light unto my Path.* The *New Testament* is so full of this Language, and the Contents of it are every where so conformable to it, that I shall refer the Reader to the particular Discussion of the Whole in the second Discourse.

CHAP. IV.

Objections *answered, drawn from the* Pravity *of Humane Reason.*

There remains one Objection yet, upon which some lay a mighty Stress, tho it's like to do them little Service. Granting, say they, the *Gospel* to be as reasonable as you pretend, yet *corrupt and deprav'd Reason can neither discern nor receive Divine Verities.* Ay, but that proves not Divine Verities to be contrary to *sound Reason.* But they maintain that *no Man's Reason is sound.* Wherefore I hope so to state this Question, as to cut off all Occasion of Dispute from judicious and peaceable Men. *Reason* taken for the Principle of Discourse in us, or more particularly for *that Faculty every one has of judging of his Idea's according to their Agreement or Disagreement, and so of loving what seems good unto him, and hating what he thinks evil: Reason,* I say, in this Sense is whole and entire in every one whose Organs are not accidentally indisposed. 'Tis from it that we are accounted Men; and we could neither inform others, nor receive Improvement our selves any more than *Brutes* without it.

But if by *Reason* be understood a constant right Use of these Faculties, *viz. If a Man never judges but according to clear Per-*

*ceptions, desires nothing but what is truly good for him, nor
avoids but what is certainly evil:* Then, I confess, it is extremely
corrupt. We are too prone to frame wrong Conceptions, and as
erroneous Judgments of things. We generally covet what flatters
our Senses, without distinguishing noxious from innocent Pleas-
ures; and our Hatred is as partial. We gratify our Bodies so
much as to meditate little, and think very grossly of spiritual
or abstracted Matters. We are apt to indulge our Inclinations,
which we term *to follow Nature* [1 Cor. 2. 14]: so that the
natural Man, that is, he that gives the swing to his Appetites,
counts Divine Things mere Folly, calls *Religion* a feverish Dream
of superstitious Heads, or a politick Trick invented by Statesmen to awe the credulous Vulgar. For as *they that walk after
the Flesh mind the things thereof,* so *their carnal Wisdom is
Enmity against God* [Rom. 8. 5, 7]. *Sin easily besets us* [Heb.
12. 1]. *There is a Law in our Members* or Body, *warring against
the Law of our Minds* [Rom. 7. 23] or Reason. And *when we
would do Good Evil is present with us* [Ver. 21]. If thus we
become stupid and unfit for earthly Speculations, *how shall we
believe when we are told of heavenly things?* [Joh. 3. 12].

But these Disorders are so far from being *Reason,* that nothing
can be more directly contrary to it. We lie under no necessary
Fate of sinning. There is no Defect in our Understandings but
those of our own Creation, that is to say, *vicious Habits easily
contracted, but difficulty reformed.* 'Tis just with us as with the
Drunkard, whose *I cannot give over Drinking* is a deliberate *I
will not.* For upon a Wager, or for a Reward, he can forbear
his Cups a Day, a Month, a Year, according as the Consideration
of the Value or Certainty of the expected Gain does influence
him. *Let no Man therefore say when he is tempted, I am tempted
of God: For as God cannot be tempted to Evil, so neither tempt-
eth he any Man: But every Man is tempted when he is drawn
away, and entic'd of his own Lust* [Jam. 1. 13, 14].

Supposing a natural Impotency to reason well, we could no
more be liable to Condemnation for not keeping the Commands
of God than those to whom *the Gospel* was never revealed for
not believing on *Christ: For how shall they call on him in whom
they have not believed? and how shall they believe in him of
whom they have not heard?* [Rom. 10. 14]. Were our reasoning

Faculties imperfect, or we not capable to employ them rightly, there could be no Possibility of our understanding one another in Millions of things, where the stock of our Idea's should prove unavoidably unequal, or our Capacities different. But 'tis the Perfection of our *Reason* and *Liberty* that makes us deserve Rewards and Punishments. We are perswaded that all our Thoughts are entirely free, we can expend the Force of Words, compare Ideas, distinguish clear from obscure Conceptions, suspend our Judgments about Uncertainties, and yield only to Evidence. In a word, the Deliberations we use about our Designs, and the Choice to which we determine our selves at last, do prove us the free Disposers of all our Actions. Now what is *sound Reason* except this be it? Doubtless it is. And no *Evangelical* or other knowable Truth can prove insuperable or monstrous to him that uses it after this manner. But when we abuse it against it self, and enslave it to our debauch'd Imaginations, it is averse from all Good. We are so habituated, I confess, to precarious and hasty Conclusions, that without great Constancy and Exercise we cannot recover our innate Freedom, *nor do well, having accustom'd our selves so much to Evil* [Jer. 13. 23]. But tho' 'tis said in *Scripture*, that *we will neither know nor understand;* 'tis there also said, that we may *amend our Ways, turn from our Iniquity,* and *choose Life.* Encouragements are proposed to such as do so. . . .

The History and Signification of Mystery in the Writings of the Gentiles.

What is meant by *Reason* we have already largely discours'd; but to understand aright what the word *Mystery* imports, we must trace the Original of it as far back as the Theology of the ancient *Gentiles,* whereof it was a considerable Term. *Those Nations, who* (as *Paul* elegantly describes them) *professing themselves wise, became Fools; who chang'd the Glory of the incorruptible God into the Image and Likeness of curruptible Man, of Birds, of Beasts, and creeping things; who turned the Truth of God into a Lie, and worshipped the Creature as well as* (and sometimes more than) *the Creator:* Those Nations, I say, asham'd or afraid to exhibit their *Religion* naked to the view

of all indifferently, disguis'd it with various Ceremonies, Sacrifices, Plays, &c. making the superstitious People believe that
admirable things were adumbrated by these Externals. The
Priests, but very rarely, and then obscurely, taught in publick,
pretending the Injunctions of their *Divinities* to the contrary,
lest their Secrets, forsooth, should be expos'd to the Profanation
of the Ignorant, or Violation of the Impious. They perform'd the
highest Acts of their Worship, consisting of ridiculous, obscene,
or inhumane Rites, in the inmost Recesses of *Temples* or *Groves*
consecrated for that purpose: And it was inexpiable Sacrilege
for any to enter these but such as had a special Mark and Privilege, or as much as to ask Questions about what passed in them.
All the Excluded were for that Reason stil'd *the Profane,* as
those not in Orders with us *the Laity.*

But the cunning *Priests,* who knew how to turn every thing to
their own Advantage, thought fit to *initiate* or instruct certain
Persons in the Meaning of their Rites. They gave out that such
as died *uninitiated* wallow'd in infernal Mire, whilst the Purified
and *Initiated* dwelt with the Gods; which as well increas'd their
Veneration for, as a Desire of enjoying so great a Happiness.
The *Initiated,* after some Years Preparation to make them value
what cost so much Time and Patience, were devoutly sworn
never to discover what they saw or heard, tho they might discourse of them amongst themselves, lest too great a Constraint
should tempt them to blab the Secret. And so religiously they
kept this Oath, that some of them, after their Conversion to
Christianity, could hardly be brought to declare what passed at
their *Initiation* in *Gentilism.* The *Athenians* thought no Tor-
ments exquisite enough to punish *Diagoras* the Philosopher, for
divulging their *Mysteries;* and not content to brand him with
Atheism for laughing at their Weakness, they promis'd a Talent
as a Reward to any that should kill him. 'Twas Death to say
Adonis was a Man; some suffer'd upon that Account: And many
were torn in pieces at the *Orgies* of *Bacchus,* for their unadvis'd
Curiosity.

Credible Authors report, that the *Priests* confess'd to the *Initiated* how these Mystick Representations were instituted at first
in Commemoration of some remarkable Accidents, or to the
Honour of some great Persons that oblig'd the World by their

Vertues and useful Inventions to pay them such Acknowledgments. But let this be as it will, *Myein* in their Systems signify'd *to initiate: Myesis, Initiation: Mystes,* a Name afterwards given the *Priests,* denoted the Person *to be initiated,* who was call'd an *Epopt* when admitted; and *Mystery* the *Doctrine in which he was initiated.* As there were several Degrees, so there were different sorts of *Mysteries.* The most famous were the *Samothracian,* the *Eleusinian,* the *Egyptian,* and those of *Bacchus,* commonly known by the Name of *Orgies;* tho the word is sometimes put for any of the former.

From what has been said it is clear, that they understood by *Mystery* in those Days *a thing intelligible of it self, but so vail'd by others, that it could not be known without special Revelation.* I need not add, that in all the *Greek* and *Roman* Authors it is constantly put, as a very vulgar Expression, for any thing sacred or profane that is designedly kept secret, or accidentally obscure. And this is the common Acceptation of it still: for when we cannot see clearly into a Business, we say it is a *Mystery* to us; and that an obscure or perplex'd Discourse is very *mysterious. Mysteries* of State, Sciences and Trades, run all in the same Notion.

But many not denying what is so plain, yet being strongly inclin'd out of Ignorance or Passion to maintain what was first introduc'd by the Craft or Superstition of their Forefathers, will have some *Christian Doctrines* to be still *mysterious* in the second Sense of the Word, that is, *inconceivable in themselves however clearly reveal'd.* They think a long Prescription will argue it Folly in any to appear against them, and indeed Custom has made it dangerous. But, slighting so mean Considerations, if I can demonstrate that in the New Testament *Mystery* is always us'd in the first Sense of the Word, or that of the *Gentiles,* viz. *for things naturally very intelligible, but so cover'd by figurative Words or Rites, that Reason could not discover them without special Revelation;* and that the Vail is actually taken away; then it will manifestly follow that the Doctrines so reveal'd cannot now be properly called *Mysteries.*

This is what I hope to perform in the Sequel of this Section, to the entire Satisfaction of those sincere Christians more concern'd for the Truth than the old or gainful Opinion. Yet I

must first remove out of my way certain common Places of
cavilling, with which, not only the raw Beginners of the most
implicite Constitution raise a great Dust upon all Occasions, tho
not able to speak of any thing pertinently when jostl'd out of
the beaten Road; but truly their venerable Teachers are not
asham'd sometimes to play at this small Game, which, they
know, rather amuses the Prejudic'd of their own side, than edifies
the Adversaries of any sort. I wish there were more even of a
well-meaning Zeal without Knowledg, than of Art or Cunning
in this Conduct.

When, why, and by whom were MYSTERIES brought into Christianity.

The End of the LAW being Righteousness [Rom. 10. 4],
JESUS CHRIST came not to destroy, but to fulfil it [Mat.
5. 17]: for he fully and clearly preach'd the purest Morals, he
taught that reasonable Worship, and those just Conceptions of
Heaven and Heavenly Things, which were more obscurely signifi'd
or design'd by the Legal Observations. So having stripp'd the
Truth of all those external Types and Ceremonies which made it
difficult before, he rendered it easy and obvious to the meanest
Capacities. His Disciples and Followers kept to this Simplicity
for some considerable time, tho very early divers Abuses began
to get footing amongst them. The converted *Jews,* who continu'd
mighty fond of their *Levitical* Rites and Feasts, would willingly
retain them and be Christians too. Thus what at the Beginning
was but only tolerated in weaker Brethren, became afterwards
a part of *Christianity* it self, under the Pretence of *Apostolick*
Prescription or Tradition.

But this was nothing compar'd to the Injury done to Religion
by the *Gentiles:* who, as they were proselyted in greater Numbers than the *Jews,* so the Abuses they introduc'd were of more
dangerous and universal Influence. They were not a little scan-
daliz'd at the plain Dress of the *Gospel,* with the wonderful
Facility of the Doctrines it contain'd, having been accustom'd
all their Lives to the pompous Worship and secret *Mysteries* of
Deities without Number. The *Christians* on the other hand were

careful to remove all Obstacles lying in the way of the *Gentiles.* They thought the most effectual way of gaining them over to their side was by compounding the Matter, which led them to unwarrantable Compliances, till at length they likewise set up for *Mysteries.* Yet not having the least Precedent for any Ceremonies from the *Gospel,* excepting *Baptism* and the *Supper,* they strangely disguiz'd and transform'd these by adding to them the Pagan Mystick Rites: They administred them with the strictest Secrecy; and, to be inferiour to their Adversaries in no Circumstance, they permitted none to assist at them, but such as were antecedently prepar'd or *initiated.* And to inspire their *Catechumens* with most ardent Desires of Participation, they gave out that what was so industriously hid were *tremendous* and *unutterable Mysteries.*

Thus lest *Simplicity,* the noblest Ornament of the Truth, should expose it to the Contempt of Unbelievers, *Christianity* was put upon an equal Level with the *Mysteries* of *Ceres,* or the *Orgies* of *Bacchus.* Foolish and mistaken Care! as if the most impious Superstitions could be sanctifi'd by the Name of *Christ.* But such is always the Fruit of prudential and condescending Terms of Conversion in Religion, whereby the Number and not the Sincerity of Professors is mainly intended.

When once the *Philosophers* thought it their Interest to turn *Christians,* Matters grew every Day worse and worse: for they not only retain'd the Air, the Genius, and sometimes the Garb of their several Sects, but most of their erroneous Opinions too. And while they pretended to imploy their *Philosophy* in Defence of *Christianity,* they so confounded them together, that what before was plain to every one, did now become intelligible only to the Learned, who made it still less evident by their Litigious Disputes and vain Subtilties. We must not forget that the *Philosophers* were for making no meaner a Figure among the *Christians* than they did formerly among the Heathens; but this was what they could not possibly effect, without rendring every thing abstruse by Terms of otherwise, and so making themselves sole Masters of the Interpretation.

These Abuses became almost incurable, when the supreme Magistrate did openly countenance the *Christian* Religion. Multitudes then profess'd themselves of the Emperor's Perswasion, only to make their Court and mend their Fortunes by it, or to preserve those Places and Preferments whereof they were posses'd. These continu'd *Pagans* in their Hearts; and it may be easily imagin'd that they carri'd all their old Prejudices along with them into a Religion which they purely embrac'd out of Politick Considerations: And so it constantly happens, when the Conscience is forc'd and not perswaded, which was a while after the Case of these *Heathens*.

The zealous Emperors erected stately Churches, and converted the Heathen Temples, Sanctuaries, Fanes or Chappels, to the Use of *Christians,* after a previous Expiation, and placing the Sign of the *Cross* in them to assure their Possession to *Christ*. All their Endowments, with the Benefices of the *Priests, Flamens, Augurs,* and the whole sacred Tribe, were appropriated to the *Christian Clergy*. Nay their very Habits, as *white Linen Stoles, Mitres,* and the like, were retain'd, to bring those, as was pretended, to an imperceptible Change, who could not be reconcil'd to the *Christian* Simplicity and Poverty. But indeed the Design at bottom was to introduce the Riches, Pomp and Dignities of the *Clergy* which immediately succeeded.

Things being in this Condition, and the Rites of *Baptism* and the *Supper* being very sensibly augmented, it will not be amiss before I pass further to lay down a short Parallel of the antient Heathen and new-coin'd Christian *Mysteries*. And I shall endeavour so to do it, as to make it evident they were one in Nature, however different in their Subjects.

First, Their Terms were exactly the same without any Alteration. . . .

Secondly, The Preparatives to their Initiations were the same. . . .

Thirdly, The *Christians* kept their *Mysteries* as secret as the *Heathens* did theirs. . . .

Fourthly, The *Fathers* were extremely cautious not to speak intelligibly of their *Mysteries* before Unbelievers or the Catechumens; whence you frequently meet in their Writings with these or the like Expressions, *The Initiated know, the Initiated understand what I say*. . . .

Fifthly, The Steps and Degrees in both their Initiations are the same. . . .

I could draw out this Parallel much larger, but here's enough to shew *how Christianity became mysterious,* and how so divine an Institution did, through the Craft and Ambition of *Priests* and *Philosophers,* degenerate into mere *Paganism.*

Mystery prevail'd very little in the first Hundred or Century of Years after *Christ;* but in the second and third, it began to establish it self by *Ceremonies.* To *Baptism* were then added the tasting of Milk and Honey, the Sign of the Cross, a white Garment, &c. There was quickly after a farther Accession of Questions and Answers, of antecedent Fastings and Watchings, anointing, kissing, and set times of Administration. Next were added Injection of Salt and Wine into the Mouths of the Baptiz'd, and a second Unction, with Imposition of Hands: But in later times there was no end of Lights, Exorcisms, Exsufflations, and many other Extravagancies of Heathen Original. From this Source sprang not only the Belief of *Omens, Presages, Apparitions,* and other vulgar Observations among Christians; but also *Images, Altars, Musick,* Dedications of Churches, and in them distinct Places for the Laity, (as they speak) and the Clergy: for there is nothing like these in the Writings of the Apostles, but they are all plainly contain'd in the Books of the Gentiles, and was the Substance of their Worship.

All the Rites of the *Supper,* too tedious to particularize, were introduc'd by degrees after the same manner. So by indeavouring to make the plainest things in the World appear *mysterious,* their very Nature and Use were absolutely perverted and destroyed, and are not yet fully restor'd by the purest Reformations in *Christendom.*

Now their own Advantage being the Motive that put the Primitive *Clergy* upon reviving *Mystery,* they quickly erected themselves by its Assistance into a separate and politick Body, tho not so soon into their various Orders and Degrees. For in the two first Centuries we meet with no *sub-Deacons, Readers,* or the like; much less with the Names or Dignities of *Popes, Cardinals, Patriarchs, Metropolitans, Archbishops, Primates, Suffragans, Archdeacons, Deans, Chancellors, Vicars,* or their numerous Dependants and Retinue. But in small time *Mystery* made way for those and several other Usurpations upon Mankind, under pretence of *Labourers in the Lord's Vineyard.*

The Decrees or Constitutions concerning *Ceremonies* and *Discipline,* to increase the Splendor of this new State, did strangely affect or stupify the Minds of the ignorant People; and made them believe they were in good earnest Mediators between God and Men, that could fix Sanctity to certain Times, Places, Persons or Actions. By this Means the *Clergy* were able to do any thing; they engross'd at length the sole Right of interpreting *Scripture,* and with it claim'd *Infallibility,* to their body.

This is the true Origin and Progress of the *Christian Mysteries;* and we may observe how great a share of their Establishment is owing to *Ceremonies.* These never fail to take off the Mind from the Substance of *Religion,* and lead Men into dangerous Mistakes: for *Ceremonies* being easily observ'd, every one thinks himself religious enough that exactly performs them. But there is nothing so naturally opposite as *Ceremony* and *Christianity.* The latter discovers Religion naked to all the World, and the former delivers it under mystical Representations of a merely arbitrary Signification.

It is visible then that Ceremonies perplex instead of explaining; but supposing they made things easier, then that would be the best Religion which had most of them, for they are generally, and may all be made, equally significative. A Candle put into the Hand of the *Baptiz'd,* to denote the Light of the Gospel, is every whit as good a *Ceremony* as to make the Sign of the Cross in token of owning Christ for their Master and Saviour. Wine, Milk and Honey signify spiritual Nourishment, Strength and Gladness, as well as standing at the *Gospel* betokens our Readiness to hear or profess it.

In short, there's no degree of *Enthusiasm* higher than placing Religion in such Fooleries; nor any thing so base as by these fraudulent Arts to make the *Gospel* of no effect, unless as far as it serves a Party. But I shall have a better Occasion of exhausting the Subject of *Ceremonies* elsewhere. I treat of 'em here only as they made up the *Gentile Mysteries,* and were afterwards brought in to constitute those of the *Christians.* But as the vast Multitudes of the latter rendred all secret Rites almost impossible, so to preserve the *Mystery*, things were purposely made downright unintelligible. In this Point our pretended *Christians* outdid all the *Mysteries* of the *Heathens;* for the Honour of these might be destroy'd by Discovery, or the babbling Tongue of any initiated Person: But the new *Mysteries* were securely plac'd above the Reach of all Sense and Reason.

A Discourse of Free-Thinking*

Anthony Collins

John Toland's aggressive polemics had lent deism, if not re-spectability, at least visibility. Defenders of Christianity went into action, and published literally scores of refutations. These refutations fall, broadly speaking, into two classes: first, there are the orthodox defenses of Christianity, supposing man's rea-son essentially feeble, and bold inquiry into religion an impiety. These defenders thought deism simply a wicked manifestation of irreligion, the latest of Satan's many incursions in this world; they were apt to hold Latitudinarian divines like Tillotson or Latitudinarian philosophers like Locke largely responsible for the rise of this new mode of unbelief. And secondly, there were the rationalist philosophers, stung by the charges of the deists that Christianity even as practiced in the Anglican Church was super-stitious, ready to give up most beliefs and practices as unim-portant or unnecessary, but insistent upon the need for special revelation, the truth of at least a few miracles, and the special status of Jesus Christ.

Powerful as many of these refutations were, they did not slow deist speculation in any way. Indeed, it enlisted some respectable allies, notably the Earl of Shaftesbury (1671-1713), essentially a theist with profound interest in the Platonic philosophy. He did not think of himself as a deist; in his major collection of essays, the Characteristics of Men, Manners, Opinions, Times etc. *(1711), he expended considerable disdain on these "free-thinkers" who are all libertines at heart. Yet in his own religious teaching he emphasized man's right to self-realization, posited an inner and wholly natural sense of morality, repudiated original sin, and explained recourse to miraculous explanations of events as a psychological need. Shaftesbury was a deist in fact, if not in*

* The passages that follow have been taken from *A Discourse of Free-Thinking, Occasion'd by the Rise and Growth of a Sect Call'd Free-Thinkers* (1713), pp. 32-56, 99-122.

78

name: he was anticlerical in the deists' way, ridiculed super-
natural tales in their way, maligned "enthusiasts" in their way,
and, above all, developed an ethical system that dispensed en-
tirely with religious sanctions. With his elegant, perhaps rather
feminine style, and his shrewd wit, Shaftesbury was a widely
read and deeply influential writer.[1]

It was in this complex atmosphere that Anthony Collins openly
professed himself a free-thinker. The friend of Locke, and, like
Toland, Locke's disciple, Collins braved the most scurrilous polemicists on the Christian side—formidable controversialists like
the classicist Richard Bentley—and survived to return to the attack. In addition to his main book, A Discourse of Free-Thinking; Occasion'd by the Rise and Growth of a Sect Call'd Free-
Thinkers (1713), Collins' chief publications were the relatively
early Priestcraft in Perfection (1709), a tract at once anticlerical
and rhapsodic about natural religion, and his last major work, A
Discourse on the Ground and Reason of the Christian Religion
(1724), in which he scattered his shots across the entire front
of controversy: The Old Testament is a collection of improbable tales; Judaism is an evil and all-too-influential superstition;
the early Christians disagreed on all important issues; the Fathers
of the Church defrauded their gullible followers. But more important, Collins attacked the value of the prophecies, which had
long been regarded as a powerful argument in behalf of Christianity. Some Old Testament prophecies are clear, but then it can
be shown that these were never fulfilled; most Old Testament
prophecies, however, are obscure, and Christian apologists have
used this obscurity to interpret them in an allegorical way, claiming that the life of Christ somehow fulfills the dark predictions
of the prophets. But, Collins insisted, an allegorical interpretation can make anything out of anything, and therefore can have
little logical force.

Collins' Discourse of Free-Thinking *does not deal with the
argument against prophecies, but it is important in its spirited
defense of untrammeled inquiry into religious questions: this*

---

[1] While Shaftesbury is a complicated figure, I here find myself in
general agreement with John Orr's straightforward interpretation
of Shaftesbury's religious position. See *English Deism: Its Roots
and Its Fruits,* pp. 122-129.

freedom, Collins argues against his many critics, is essential pre-cisely because religious men contradict one another so fiercely, and priests of all castes are so unreliable.

The Subjects of which Men are deny'd the Right to think by the Enemys of *Free-Thinking,* are of all others those of which Men have not only *a Right to think,* but of which they are oblig'd in duty to think; *viz.* such as *of the Nature and Attributes of the Eternal Being* or *God, of the Truth and Authority of Books esteem'd Sacred,* and *of the Sense and Meaning of those Books;* or, in one word, *of Religious Questions.*

1*st.* A right Opinion in these matters is suppos'd by the *Enemys of Free-Thinking* to be absolutely necessary to Mens Salvation, and some Errors or Mistakes about them are suppos'd to be damnable. Now where a right Opinion is so necessary, there Men have the greatest Concern imaginable to think for themselves, as the best means to take up with the right side of the Question. For if they will not think for themselves, it remains only for them to take the Opinions they have imbib'd from their Grandmothers, Mothers or Priests, or owe to such like Accident, for granted. But taking that method, they can only be in the right by chance; whereas by Thinking and Examination, they have not only the mere accident of being in the right, but have the Evidence of things to determine them to the side of Truth: unless it be suppos'd that Men are such absurd Animals, that the most unreasonable Opinion is as likely to be admitted for true as the most reasonable, when it is judg'd of by the Reason and Understanding of Men. In that case indeed it will follow, That Men can be under no Obligation to think of these matters. But then it will likewise follow, That they can be under no Obligation to concern themselves about Truth and Falshood in any Opinions. For if Men are so absurd, as not to be able to distinguish between Truth and Falshood, Evidence and no Evidence, what pretence is there for Mens having any Opinions at all? Which yet none judg so necessary as the Enemys of *Free-Thinking.*

2*dly.* If the surest and best means of arriving at Truth lies in *Free-Thinking,* then the whole Duty of Man with respect to Opinions lies only in *Free-Thinking.* Because he who *thinks freely* does his best towards being in the right, and consequently does all that God, who can require nothing more of any Man than that he should do his best, can require of him. And should he prove mistaken in any Opinions, he must be as acceptable to God as if he receiv'd none but right Opinions. . . .

On the other side, the whole Crime of Man, with respect to Opinions, must lie in his not *thinking freely*. He who is in the right by accident only, and does but suppose himself to be so without any *Thinking*, is really in a dangerous state, as having taken no pains and used no endeavours towards being in the right, and consequently as having no Merit; nay, as being on the same foot with the most stupid *Papist* and *Heathen*. For when once Men refuse or neglect to think, and take up their Opinions upon trust, they do in effect declare they would have been *Papists* or *Heathens*, had they had *Popish* or *Heathen* Priests for their *Guides*, or *Popish* or *Heathen* Grandmothers to have taught them their Catechisms.

3dly. Superstition is an Evil, which either by the means of Education, or the natural Weakness of Men, oppresses almost all Mankind. And how terrible an Evil it is, is well describ'd by the antient Philosophers and Poets. TULLY says, *If you give way to Superstition, it will ever haunt and plague you. If you go to a Prophet, or regard Omens; if you sacrifice or observe the Flight of Birds; if you consult an Astrologer or Haruspex; if it thunders or lightens, or any place is consum'd with Lightning, or such-like Prodigy happens (as it is necessary some such often should) all the Tranquillity of the Mind is destroy'd. And Sleep it self, which seems to be an Asylum and Refuge from all Trouble and Uneasiness, does by the aid of Superstition increase your Troubles and Fears.*

Horace ranks Superstition with Vice; and as he makes the Happiness of Man in this Life to consist in the practice of Virtue and Freedom from Superstition, so he makes the greatest Misery of this Life to consist in being vicious and superstitious. *You are not covetous,* says he; *that's well: But are you as free from all other Vices? Are you free from Ambition, excessive Anger, and the Fear of Death? Are you so much above* Superstition, *as to laugh at all Dreams, panick Fears, Miracles, Witches, Ghosts, and Prodigys?*

This was the state of Superstition among the Antients; but since Uncharitableness and damning to all eternity for Trifles, has (in opposition both to Reason and Revelation) come into the World, the Evil of Superstition is much increas'd, and Men are now under greater Terrors and Uneasiness of Mind than they possibly could be when they thought they hazarded less.

Now there is no just Remedy to this universal Evil but *Free-Thinking*. By that alone can we understand the true Causes of things, and by consequence the Unreasonableness of all superstitious Fears. *Happy is the Man,* says the Divine VIRGIL, *who has discover'd the Causes of Things, and is thereby cured of all kind of Fears, even of Death it self, and all the Noise and Din of Hell.* For by *Free-Thinking* alone Men are capable of knowing, that a perfectly Good, Just, Wise and Powerful Being made and governs the World; and from this Principle they know, that he can require nothing of Men in any Country or Condition of Life, but that whereof he has given them an opportunity of being convinc'd by Evidence and Reason in the Place where they are, and in that Condition of Life to which Birth or any other Chance has directed them; that an honest and rational Man can have no just reason to fear any thing from him: nay, on the contrary, must have so great a Delight and Satisfaction in believing such a Being exists, that he can much better be suppos'd to fear lest no such Being should exist, than to fear any harm from him. And lastly, That God being incapable of having any addition made either to his Power or Happiness, and wanting nothing, can require nothing of Men for his own sake, but only for Man's sake; and consequently, that all Actions and Speculations which are of no use to Mankind, [as for instance, Singing or Dancing, or wearing of Habits, or Observation of Days, or eating or drinking, or slaughtering of Beasts (in which things the greatest part of the Heathen Worship consisted) or the Belief of *Transubstantiation* or *Consubstantiation,* or of any Doctrines not taught by the *Church of England*] either signify nothing at all with God, or else displease him, but can never render a Man more acceptable to him.

By means of all this, a Man may possess his Soul in peace, as having an expectation of enjoying all the good things which

God can bestow, and no fear of any future Misery or Evil from his hands; and the very worst of his State can only be, that he is pleasantly deceiv'd.

Whereas superstitious Men are incapable of believing in a perfectly just and good God. They make him talk to all Mankind from corners, and consequently require things of Men under the Sanction of Misery in the next World, of which they are incapable of having any convincing Evidence that they come from him. They make him (who *equally beholds all the Dwellers upon earth*) to have favourite Nations and People, without any Consideration of Merit. They make him put other Nations under Disadvantages without any Demerit. And so they are more properly to be stil'd *Demonists* than *Theists*. No wonder therefore if such Wretches should be so full of Fears of the Wrath of God, that they are sometimes tempted (with the Vicious) to wish there was no God at all; a Thought so unnatural and absurd, that even *Speculative Atheists* would abhor it. These Men have no quiet in their own Minds; they rove about in search of *saving Truth* thro the dark Corners of the Earth, and are so foolish as to hope to find it (if I may so say) hid under the Sands of *Africa*, where *Cato* scorn'd to look for it: and neglecting what God speaks plainly to the whole World, take up with what they suppose he has communicated to a few; and thereby believe and practice such things, in which they can never have Satisfaction. For suppose Men take up with a Religion which consists in Dancing or Musick, or such-like Ceremonys, or in useless and unintelligible Speculations; how can they be assur'd they believe and perform as they ought? What Rule can such Men have to know whether other Ceremonys, and useless and unintelligible Speculations, may not be requir'd of them instead of those they perform and believe? And how can they be sure that they believe rightly any unintelligible Speculations? Here is a foundation laid for nothing but endless Scruples, Doubts, and Fears. Wherefore I conclude, that every one, out of regard to his own Tranquillity of Mind, which must be disturb'd as long as he has any Seeds of Superstition, is oblig'd to *think freely* on *Matters of Religion*.

4*thly*. The infinite number of Pretenders in all Ages to Revelations from Heaven, supported by Miracles, containing new No-

tions of the Deity, new Doctrines, new Commands, new Ceremonys, and new Modes of Worship, make thinking on the foregoing Heads absolutely necessary, if a Man be under an obligation to listen to any Revelation at all. For how shall any Man
distinguish between the true Messenger from Heaven and the
Impostor, but by considering the Evidence produc'd by the one,
as *freely* as of the other?

5thly. We have here in *England* a *Society* supported by the
Encouragement of her *most Excellent Majesty,* and the Con-
tributions of many *Divines* and *Ladys* of our *Establish'd Church,*
in effect for the *Propagation* of *Free-Thinking* in matters of Religion throughout the World; and whose Design supposes that it
is all Mens Duty to *think freely* about matters of Religion. For
how can the *Society for propagating the Gospel in foreign Parts*
hope to have any effect on Infidel Nations, without first ac-
quainting them that it is their duty to *think freely* both on the
Notions of God and Religion, which they have receiv'd from
their Ancestors, or which are *establish'd by Law* among them,
and on those new Notions of God and Religion brought to them
by the *Missionarys* of the *Church of England?* Can it be suppos'd, that our *Missionarys* would begin with telling 'em, that
they ought not to *think freely* of their own, or our Religion; or
that after they have by the means of *Free-Thinking* embrac'd
our Religion, they ought then to cease from *Free-Thinking?*
This were to proceed very inconsistently in the Work of Conversion, while no other Arms but Reason and Evidence were
made use of to convert. On the contrary, every *Missionary*
must as a first Principle insist on the Duty of *Free-Thinking,*
in order to be hearken'd to by them. Nay, should the *King of
Siam* (or any other infidel Prince) in return for the Favour of
our Endeavours to convert him and his Kingdom to our Religion, desire to send us a parcel of his *Talapoins* (so the Priests
of *Siam* are call'd) to convert us to the *Religion by Law establish'd* in *Siam;* I cannot see but that our *Society for propagating
the Gospel,* and all the Contributors and Well-wishers to it,
must acknowledg the *King's* Request to be highly reasonable,
and perfectly of a-piece with their own Project; and particularly
must allow to the King of *Siam,* that it is as much the Duty of
the Members of the Church of *England* to *think freely* on what

the *Missionary Talapoins* shall propose to them, as it is the Duty
of the Members of the Church of *Siam* to *think freely* on what
shall be propos'd by the *Missionary Priests* of *England:* And
therefore no doubt all they who sincerely desir'd the Conviction
of the *Siamese,* would give their *Missionarys* the same Encouragement here, which we expect for ours in *Siam.* The Institution
therefore of this *Society* supposes *Free-Thinking* in matters of
Religion to be the Duty of all Men on the face of the Earth.
And upon that account I cannot sufficiently commend the
Project.

And Oh! that the proper Persons were but employ'd for the
Execution of so glorious a Design! . . . We might then hope
to see blessed Days, the *Doctrine and Discipline of the Church
of England* triumph throughout the World, and Faction cease
at home; as by the means of the others our Arms triumph
abroad, and we securely take our rest at night, and travel by
day unmolested.

And no doubt likewise, but it would be as beneficial to the
Kingdom of *Siam,* to have a select number annually taken out of
their vast Body of *Talapoins.*

6*thly.* As there can be no reasonable Change of Opinions
among Men, no quitting of any old Religion, no Reception of
any new Religion, nor believing any Religion at all, but by means
of *Free-Thinking;* so the Holy Scriptures agreeably to Reason,
and to the Design of our *Blessed Saviour* of establishing his
Religion throughout the whole Universe, imply every where
and press in many places the Duty of *Free-Thinking.*

The Design of the *Gospel* was, by preaching, to set all Men
upon *Free-Thinking,* that they might think themselves out of
those Notions of God and Religion which were every where
establish'd by Law, and receive an *unknown God* and *an unknown Religion* on the Evidence the *Apostles,* or first Messen-
gers, produc'd to convince them. And accordingly the Apostles
requir'd nothing to be receiv'd on their Authority, without an
antecedent Proof given of their Authority. St. PAUL even in his
Epistles, which are all written to Men who were already *Christians,* offers many Arguments for their Confirmation in the *true
Faith,* with respect to all the parts of the *Christian Religion.*
Whereby he made them, and all his Readers for ever Judges of

their Force: for whoever reasons, lays aside all Authority, and endeavours to force your Assent by Argument alone. St. PAUL likewise went frequently into the Synagogues of the *Jews,* and *reason'd* [Acts 17. 2, 3] with them; which was not only putting the *Jews* upon *Free-Thinking* on matters of Religion, but taking (according to the present Notions of *Christians*) a very extraordinary step to put them upon *Free-Thinking.* For should WILLIAM PENN the *Quaker,* or other religious Person differing from the *Establish'd Church,* come to *St. Paul's* during the time of *Divine Service* to *reason* with the *Court of Aldermen, Preacher,* and *Singing-Men;* or Mr. WHISTON into the *Lower House of Convocation,* to *reason* with them; it is certain, that pursuant to the false Notions which now universally prevail, the *one* would be treated as a *Madman* and *Fanatick,* and the other as a *Disturber of the Proceedings of the Holy Synod,* which assumes a right to determine without *Reasoning* with the Person whose Opinions they condemn.

Our Saviour particularly commands us to *search the Scriptures* [Joh. 5. 39], that is, to endeavour to find out their true meaning. And for fear we should surrender our Judgments to our Fathers, and Mothers, or Church-Rulers, or Preachers, he bids us *take heed what we hear* [Mar. 4. 24], and *whom* we *hear* [Luk. 8. 18], and to *beware of their Doctrine* [Mat. 16. 12]. And *why,* says he, *even of your selves judg ye not what is right? If a Man come to me, and hate not his Father and Mother, he cannot be my Disciple.* [Luke 12. 56, 57. 14. 26. Mat. 19. 29.] And he commanded his own *Disciples* not to *be call'd Rabbi* nor *Masters. . . .* And indeed whoever considers, that all the Priests upon earth were Enemys to our *Blessed Saviour* and his Gospel, and that he giving the privilege of *Infallibility* to no body besides his holy Apostles, could not be secure that any Priests would ever be otherwise; I say, he who considers this, can never think it possible for CHRIST to give so partial a Command, as to contain a Reserve in behalf of any Set of Priests, in prejudice of the general Rules of *Free-Thinking,* on which the *Gospel* was to be built, and which he so particularly laid down and inculcated.

6thly. The Conduct of the Priests, who are the chief Pretenders to be Guides to others in matters of Religion, makes *Free-Thinking* on *the Nature and Attributes of the Eternal Being or God,* on *the Authority of Scriptures,* and on *the Sense of Scriptures,* unavoidable. And to prove this, I will give you an Induction of several Particulars of their Conduct.

1*st.* It is well known that the Priests throughout the Universe are endlessly divided in Opinion about all these matters; and their Variety of Opinion is so great, as not possibly to be collected together: nay, even those kinds of Priests, with which we are more nearly concern'd, differ so much one among another on some of these heads, that it would be an impossible task to give you all their Differences. I will therefore out of this vast and spacious Field select such under each of these heads, as is most proper to affect us *Englishmen.*

(1.) As to the *Nature of the Eternal Being or God,* the antient and modern Pagan Priests had and have as many different Ideas of the Deity, as Wit, or Interest, or Folly can invent; and even the Christian Priests have been always, and still are, divided in their Notions of a Deity. Almost all the antient Priests and Fathers (who were most of them Priests) of the Christian Church conceiv'd God to be material; and several antient *Christian Priests* of *Egypt* were so gross, as to conceive him to be in the shape of Man, and from thence were call'd *Anthropomorphites.* Most of the modern Priests contend that God is *immaterial,* but they differ in their Notion of *Immateriality;* some by *Immaterial Being* understanding *extended Substance without Solidity;* and others by *Immaterial Being* understanding *unextended Being.*

If any regard is to be had to the malicious Books and Sayings of Priests one against another, several of them make the *material Universe to be the Eternal Being or God,* wherein consists the *Essence of Atheism.* . . .

As the *Christian Priests* differ about the *Nature* or *Essence of God,* so they are infinitely more divided in their Notions about his *Attributes.*

The whole difference between the *Arminians* and *Calvinists* is founded on different Notions of the Attributes of God; and this Dispute is kept up in most Christian Churches on the face of the earth. It is carry'd on in the *Romish* Church under the names of *Jansenists* and *Jesuits, Thomists* and *Molinists,* &c. It has been for near a Century last past debated among the Divines

of our Church, and is at this day between the Reverend Dr.
WHITBY and his Adversarys. Indeed the Differences among the
Priests in every Church about the *Attributes of God,* are as
numerous as the Priests who treat of the *Divine Attributes;* not
one agreeing with another in his Notions of them all. I will
therefore close this matter with one instance of a most remarkable
Difference.

It is the Opinion of many Divines, That when the Scriptures
attribute Hands, and Eyes, and Feet, and Face to God, we are
not to understand that God really has those parts, but only that
he has a power to execute all those Actions, to the effecting of
which those parts are necessary in us. And when the Scriptures
attribute such Passions to God as Anger, Pleasure, Love, Hatred,
Repentance, Revenge, and the like; the meaning is, that he will
as certainly punish the Wicked, as if he was inflam'd with the
Passion of Anger; that he will as infallibly reward the Good,
as if he had a love for them; and that when Men turn from
their Wickedness, he will suit Dispensations to them, as if he
really repented or chang'd his Mind: So that these Scripture-
Attributes belong not to God in a proper and just Sense, but
only improperly, or as the Schools speak, *analogically.* But when
the Scripture attributes to God an Understanding, Wisdom, Will,
Goodness, Holiness, Justice and Truth, these words are to be
understood strictly and properly, or in their common sense.
Dr. TILLOTSON, the late Archbishop of *Canterbury,* throughout
his Works maintains this System of the Deity. I need only cite
his words with respect to those Attributes last mention'd; his
Notions, with respect to Parts or Passions in God, being sufficiently known without any proof. He says,* *It is foolish for any
Man to pretend he cannot know what Justice, and Goodness,
and Truth in God are; for if we do not know this, it is all one
to us whether God be good or not, nor could we imitate his
Goodness; for he that imitates, endeavours to make himself
like something that he knows, and must of necessity have some
Idea of that to which he aims to be like. So that if we had no
certain and settled Notion of the Goodness, and Justice, and
Truth of God, he would be altogether an unintelligible Being;
and Religion, which consists in the Imitation of him, would be*

* *Sermons,* vol. 6, p. 15, 16.

utterly lost. Thus that *Religious* and *Free-Thinking Prelate.* But on the other side, Dr. KING the present Archbishop of *Dublin* tells us,† *That the best Representations we can make of God, are infinitely short of Truth;* That *Wisdom, Understanding, and Mercy, Foreknowledg, Predestination, and Will, when ascrib'd to God, are not to be taken properly* [P. 7, 8]. Again, That *Justice and Virtue* (and by consequence all the moral Attributes of God) *are not to be understood to signify the same thing when apply'd to God and Man;* and *that they are of so different a nature from what they are in us, and so superiour to all that we can conceive, that there is no more likeness between them, than between our Hand and God's Power* [P. 34, 35]. But all these Attributes, according to his *Grace,* are to be understood in the same manner, as *when Men ascribe Hands, and Eyes, and Feet to God;* or as when *Men ascribe Anger, Love, Hatred, Revenge, Repentance, changing Resolutions, and in the same improper Analogical Sense.* So that as his Grace of *Canterbury* would define God to be a *Being without Parts and Passions, Holy, Wise, Just, True,* and *Good;* his *Grace of* Dublin must on the contrary define God to be a *Being* not only *without Parts and Passions,* but *without Understanding, Wisdom, Will, Mercy, Holiness, Goodness,* or *Truth.*

2*dly.* The Priests throughout the World differ about Scriptures, and the Authority of Scriptures. The *Bramins* have a Book of *Scripture* call'd the *Shaster.* The *Persees* have their *Zundavastaw.* The *Bonzes* of *China* have Books written by the *Disciples of* Fo-HE, whom they call the *God and Saviour of the World, who was born to teach the way of Salvation, and to give satisfaction for all Mens Sins.* The *Talapoins* of *Siam* have a *Book of Scripture* written by SOMMONOCODOM, who, the *Siamese* say, was *born of a Virgin,* and was *the God expected by the Universe.* The *Dervizes* have their *Alchoran.* The *Rabbi's* among the *Samaritans,* who now live at *Sichem* in *Palestine,* receive the *five Books of* MOSES (the Copy whereof is very different from ours) as their Scripture; together with a *Chronicon,* or History of themselves from MOSES's time, quite different from that contain'd in the *Historical Books of the Old Testament.* This *Chronicon* is lodg'd in the publick Library of *Leyden,* and has never

† *Sermon on Divine Predest.* p. 16.

been publish'd in print. The *Rabbi's* among the common Herd
of *Jews* receive for Scripture the *four and twenty Books* of the
Old Testament. The *Priests* of the *Roman* Church, of the *English* and other Protestant Churches, receive for Scripture the
four and twenty Books of the *Old Testament,* and all the *Books
of the New Testament:* but the *Roman* receives several other
Books, call'd *Apocrypha,* as *Canonical,* which all the *Protestant
Churches* utterly reject, except the Church of *England;* which,
differently from all other Christian Churches, receives them as
half Canonical, reading some parts of them in their Churches,
and thereby excluding some Chapters of *Canonical Scripture*
from being read.

I must observe, That the *Priests* of all Christian Churches
differ among themselves in each Church about the Copys of the
same *Books of Scripture;* some reading them according to one
Manuscript, and others according to another. But the great Dispute of all, is concerning the *Hebrew* and *Septuagint,* between
which two there is a great difference; (the latter making the
World 1500 Years older than the former:) to name no other
Differences of greater or less importance.

Lastly, As the most antient Christian Churches and Priests
receiv'd several *Gospels* and *Books of Scripture* which are now
lost, such as *the Gospel according to the* Hebrews, *the Gospel
according to the* Egyptians, *the Traditions of* Matthias, *&c.* and
as not one of their Successors in the two first Centurys (whose
Works now remain) but receiv'd Books of Scripture, which are
either lost to us, or that we reject as *Apocryphal:* so the several
Sects of Christians in the *East* and in *Africa* receive at this day
some Books of Scripture, which are so far lost to us, that we
know only their Names, and others which we have and reject.

The same Books of Scripture have, among those Priests who
receive them, a very different degree of Authority; some attributing more, and others less Authority to them.

The Popish Priests contend that the Text of Scripture is so
corrupted, precarious, and unintelligible, that we are to depend
on the Authority of their Church for the true Particulars of the
Christian Religion. Others who contend for a greater Perfection
in the Text of Scripture, differ about the Inspiration of those
Books; some contending that every Thought and Word are in-

spir'd; some that the Thoughts are inspir'd, and not the Words; some that those Thoughts only are inspir'd, which relate to Fundamentals; and others that the Books were written by honest Men with great Care and Faithfulness, without any Inspiration either with respect to the Thoughts or Words.

In like manner, the *Bramins, Persees, Bonzes, Talapoins, Dervizes, Rabbi's,* and all other *Priests* who build their Religion on Books, must from the nature of things vary about Books in the same Religion, about the Inspiration, and Copys of those Books.

3*dly.* The Priests differ about the Sense and Meaning of those Books they receive as Sacred. This is evident from the great number of Sects in each Religion, founded on the Diversity of Senses put on their several Scriptures. And tho the Books of the *Old and New Testament* are the immediate Dictates of God himself, and all other *Scriptures* are the Books of Impostors; yet are the Priests of the Christian Church (like the Priests of all other Churches) not only divided into numberless Sects, on account of their different Interpretations of *them,* but even the Priests of the same Sect differ endlesly in Opinion about their Sense and Meaning. . . .

I have frequently observ'd in Conversation, that Men are more led by certain Difficulties and Objections, which they pick up, to reject what is certain and true, than they are to admit any thing for true by virtue of a proof *à priori.* Wherefore I will now consider the principal Objections I have met with, in the mouths of the Sincere, to Examination and *Free-Thinking.*

1*st.* It is objected, *That to suppose Men have a right to think on all Subjects, is to engage them in Enquirys for which they are no ways qualify'd; the Bulk of Mankind really wanting a Capacity to think justly about any Speculations: and therefore 'tis absurd to assert that Men have a right to think freely, much more that it is their Duty to think freely.* To which I answer,

1. That to assert only a bare Right in any Man to do a thing, implies a Right in him to let it alone, if he thinks fit. And therefore no Man need engage himself in any Enquirys by virtue of his Right to *think freely,* unless he judges himself sufficiently qualify'd.

2. To assert it is all Mens Duty to *think freely* on certain Subjects, engages them only in Enquirys on those Subjects, which

they who contend for the Necessity of all Mens assenting to certain Propositions, must allow all Men are qualify'd to do. For the only way to know what Opinion I ought to have in any matter, is to think about that matter; and to suppose that God requires me to believe any Opinion, and has not put into my power the means of knowing what that Opinion is, is absurd.

3. Supposing the Bulk of Mankind do want the Capacity to *think freely* on matters of Speculation, I do then allow, that *Free-Thinking* can be no Duty; and the Priests must likewise allow, that Men can be no way concern'd about Truth or Falshood in speculative matters, and that the Belief of no Opinions can be justly requir'd of them. But still the Right to *think freely* will remain untouch'd for all those who are dispos'd to *think freely*.

2dly. It is objected, *That to allow and encourage Men to think freely, will produce endless Divisions in Opinion, and by consequence Disorder in Society.* To which I answer,

1. Let any Man lay down a Rule to prevent Diversity of Opinions, which will not be as fertile of Diversity of Opinions as *Free-Thinking;* or if it prevents Diversity of Opinions, will not be a Remedy worse than the Disease; and I will yield up the Question.

2. Mere Diversity of Opinions has no tendency in nature to Confusion in Society. The *Pythagoreans, Stoicks, Scepticks, Academicks, Cynicks,* and *Stratonicks,* all existed in *Greece* at the same time, and differ'd from one another in the most important Points, *viz.* concerning the Freedom of human Actions, the Immortality and Immateriality of the Soul, the Being and Nature of the Gods, and their Government of the World: And yet no Confusion ever arose in *Greece* on account of this Diversity of Opinions. Nor did the infinite Variety of Religions and Worships among the Antients ever produce any Disorder or Confusion. Nay, so little *Polemick Divinity* was there among them, and so little mischief did the Heathen Priests do, that there are no Materials for that sort of History call'd *Ecclesiastical History.* And the true reason why no ill effect follow'd this Diversity of Opinions, was, because Men generally agreed in that mild and peaceable Principle of allowing one another to *think freely,* and to have different Opinions. Whereas had the com-

mon practice of Calumny us'd among us prevail'd among them,
or had they condemn'd one another to Fire and Faggot, Im-
prisonment and Fines in this World, and Damnation in the next,
and by these means have engag'd the Passions of the ignorant
part of Mankind in their several Partys; then Confusion, Disorder, and *every evil Work* had follow'd, as it does at this day
among those who allow no Liberty of Opinion. We may be
convinc'd of this by our own Experience. How many Disputes
are there every where among Philosophers, Physicians, and Divines; which, by the allowance of free Debate, produce no ill
effects? Further, let any man look into the History and State
of the *Turks,* and he will see the influence which their tolerating
Principles and Temper have on the Peace of their Empire. . . .
So that it is evident Matter of Fact, that a *Restraint upon
Thinking* is the cause of all the Confusion which is pretended
to arise from Diversity of Opinions, and that *Liberty of Thinking* is the Remedy for all the Disorders which are pretended
to arise from Diversity of Opinions.

3*dly.* It is objected, *That if Free-Thinking be allow'd, it is
possible some Men may think themselves into Atheism; which
is esteem'd the greatest of all Evils in Government.* To which
I answer,

1. My Lord BACON says, *The contemplative Atheist is rare:*
But many Divines maintain that there never was a real *Atheist*
in the world. And since the Matter of Fact is so uncertain as
to be made a *Problem,* there needs no provision against such a
Monster.

2. If there is any such *rare Monster* as an *Atheist,* DAVID
has given us his Character in these words, *The Fool hath said
in his heart, there is no God* [Pial. 14. 1]; that is, no one denies
the Existence of a God but some idle, unthinking, shallow Fellow. And Mr. HOBBES says, *That they who are capable of in-
specting the Vessels of Generation, and Nutrition, and not think
them made for their several Ends by an understanding Being,
ought to be esteem'd destitute of Understanding themselves.* And
my Lord BACON further judiciously remarks, *That a little Philosophy inclineth mens Minds to Atheism, but Depth in Philosophy bringeth mens Minds about to Religion.* And his Observation is confirm'd by Experience. For in ignorant Popish Coun-

trys, where *Free-Thinking* passes for a Crime, *Atheism* most abounds; for *Free-Thinking* being banish'd, it remains only for Men to take up their Religion upon trust from the Priest: which being such a Jest upon all things sacred, by making the Truths of God to depend on the various and contradictory Whimsys of interested and fallible Men; half-witted and unthinking People, who can easily see through this, conclude all alike the Priest says. So that Ignorance is the foundation of *Atheism,* and *Free-Thinking* the Cure of it. And thus tho it should be allow'd, that some Men by *Free-Thinking* may become *Atheists,* yet they will ever be fewer in number if *Free-Thinking* were permitted, than if it were restrain'd.

3. But supposing that *Free-Thinking* will produce a great number of *Atheists;* yet it is certain *they* can never be so numerous where *Free-Thinking* is allow'd, as the *Superstitious* and *Enthusiasts* will be, if *Free-Thinking* were restrain'd. And if these latter are equally or more mischievous to Society than the former, then it is better to allow of *Free-Thinking,* tho it should increase the number of *Atheists,* than by a *Restraint* of *Free-Thinking* to increase the number of *Superstitious People* and *Enthusiasts.* Now that *Enthusiasts* and *Superstitious People* are more mischievous to Society, I will prove to you in the judicious Remarks of two Men of great Authority.

My Lord BACON says, *Atheism leaves a Man to Sense, to Philosophy, to natural Piety, to Laws, to Reputation; all which may be Guides to an outward moral Vertue, tho Religion were not: But Superstition dismounts all these, and erecteth an absolute Monarchy in the Minds of Men. Therefore Atheism did never perturb States; for it maketh Men wary of themselves, as looking no further: and we see the Times inclin'd to Atheism (as the Times of* AUGUSTUS CÆSAR) *were civil Times. But Superstition hath been the Confusion of many States; and bringeth in a new* Primum Mobile *that ravisheth all the Spheres of Government.* . . .

4thly. It is objected, *That the Priests are set apart to think freely for the Laity, and are to be rely'd on, as Lawyers, Physicians, &c. are in their several Facultys.* To this I answer,

1. That no Man is excluded from studying Law or Physick, because there are several of those Professions, nor from follow-

ing his own Judgment when he is sick or in Law; nor is there any reason why a Man, who is not a Doctor in Physick or a Serjeant at Law, may not understand as much Law and Physick as either of them. In like manner, the setting Men apart for the Study of Divinity, does not exclude others from the Study of Divinity, nor from following their Judgment about a Point in Divinity, nor from knowing as much Divinity as any Doctor in Divinity. And by consequence there is no necessity to rely on any Man's Judgment, either in Law, Physick, or Divinity. . . .

2. But supposing that the Bulk of Mankind are oblig'd in matters of Law and Physick to rely on some one in those Professions, the Parallel will not hold from Law and Physick to Divinity, and the Cases are different in these following respects.

(1.) When I thro Unskilfulness in Law or Physick rely on some Lawyer or Physician, I am by no means under an Obligation implicitly to believe the Principles or Opinions upon which the one prescribes or the other acts, or so much as to know any thing in nature about them. The Physician may cure me of a Distemper, and the Lawyer may get me my Right, let my Ignorance in either Profession be ever so great: These are matters which can be transacted by a *Deputy*. Whereas in matters of Divinity I am oblig'd to believe certain Opinions my self, and can *depute* no Man to believe for me; nor will any Man's Belief save me, except my own. So that it is my Duty to think for my self in matters of Religion, and I am at liberty whether I will study Law or Physick.

(2.) Priests have no interest to lead me to true Opinions, but only to the Opinions they have listed themselves to profess, and for the most part into mistaken Opinions: For it is manifest that all Priests, except the Orthodox, are hir'd to lead Men into Mistakes. Whereas there are no Lawyers nor Physicians set apart and hir'd to defend mistaken Opinions in those Professions. And their Interest, as to Success, is the same with their *Clients* and *Patients;* but the Priests Interest is mostly different from that of the *Laity*. A *Layman* wants to know the Truth, and the *Priest* desires to have him of his Opinion.

(3.) Priests are not set apart to study Divinity, as Lawyers and Physicians are to study Law and Physick. The Priests do not study Divinity properly so call'd, but only how to maintain a certain System of Divinity. Thus the *Popish, Mahometan, Lutheran,* and *Presbyterian* Priests, study their several Systems. Whereas Physicians are not ty'd down to HIPPOCRATES, or GALEN, or PARACELSUS, but have all Nature and all Mens Observations before them, without any Obligation to subscribe implicitly to any one: nor have Lawyers any Rule, but the Law it self which lies before 'em, which they are at liberty to interpret according to its real Sense, being bound by no Atricles or Subscriptions to interpret it otherwise.

(4.) If I die thro the Conduct of a Physician, or lose my Right by the Conduct of my Lawyer, that is the worst which can befal me; but if I trust to a Priest who is in the wrong, I am suppos'd to be eternally damn'd.

3. But thirdly I answer, That supposing the Cases are parallel, no Benefit will follow to any Set of Priests in particular, nor will there be any prevention of Diversity of Opinions, or of any other of those Evils which *Free-Thinking* is suppos'd to produce. For if the Cases are parallel, then Men may chuse their own Priests, as they chuse their own Lawyers and Physicians. . . .

5thly. It is objected, *That certain Speculations (tho false) are necessary to be impos'd on Men, in order to assist the Magistrate in preserving the Peace of Society:* And *that it is therefore as reasonable to deceive Men into Opinions for their own Good, as it is in certain cases to deceive Children; and consequently it must be absurd to engage Men in thinking on Subjects where Error is useful and Truth injurious to them.* To which I answer,

1. That this is an irreligious Objection, and is so treated by CICERO in the Person of COTTA. Says he, *What do you think of those Men, who have said that the Opinion of the Existence of the immortal Gods was invented by wise Men for the publick Good; that they who would not be govern'd by Reason, might be influenc'd by Religion to do their Duty? Have not they destroy'd all Religion?*

2. I will grant the Reasoning contain'd in the *Objection* to be founded on a just Principle, *viz.* That the Good of Society is the *Rule* of whatever is to be allow'd or restrain'd; and I will likewise grant, that if Errors are useful to human Society, they ought to be impos'd: and consequently I must allow the Inference, *That Thinking ought to be restrain'd.* But then I affirm,

That the Rule is as *falsly* as it is *irreligiously* apply'd, and that both Experience and Reason demonstrate the *Imposition* of Speculations, whether true or false, to be so far from being a Benefit, that it has been and must be the greatest Mischief that has ever befel or can befal Mankind.

(1.) Lust, Covetousness, Revenge, and Ambition have in all Ages more or less plagued the World, and been the Source of great Disorders. But *Zeal* to impose Speculations has not only had the same effects in common with those Passions, but has carry'd Men to a pitch of Wickedness, which otherwise *Eye had not seen, nor Ear heard, nor had enter'd into the Heart of Man to conceive.* For what antient or modern History can parallel the *Brutality* of *Religious Zealots?* What, the numerous Massacres, Desolations, and Murders for Religion, in particular the Massacres of *France* and *Ireland,* and the Desolations and Murders committed by the *Spaniards* in the *West-Indies?* What, the complicated Wickedness and Cruelty of our *English Clergy,* whom, as Bishop TAYLOR tells us, HENRY *the Fourth, because he usurp'd the Crown, was willing by all means to endear by* murdering Hereticks, *that so he might be sure of them to all his purposes?* And what, that steddy lasting Machine of Slavery, Villany and Cruelty, the Tribunal of the *Inquisition?* The most irregular of our other Passions decay with Time, and their mischievous Effects are restrain'd by good Sense and human Policy; and we have some Passions in us, such as Pity, Good-Nature and Humanity, which help to preserve a tolerable Ballance in the human Machine. But *Religious Zeal* gathers strength with Time, bears down common Sense and Policy, leaps the bounds of natural Humanity, and vanquishes all the tender Passions. . . .

(2.) The great Charge of supporting such numbers of Men as are necessary to maintain Impositions, is a Burden upon Society which was never felt on any other occasion. For I suppose it will be allow'd me, that the Revenues belonging to the Orders of *Priests, Monks,* and *Fryars* in *Popish Countrys,* are a greater Tax on the Subject, and have introduc'd a greater degree of Poverty, than has ever been felt from any Lay-Tyrants or Conquerors: for the latter have been contented with temporary *Plunder* only, without concerning themselves how to find out ways to make Mankind Beggars for ever. The Charge alone

therefore of supporting such a number of Ecclesiasticks, is a
great Evil to Society, tho it should be suppos'd the *Ecclesiasticks*
themselves were employ'd in the most innocent manner imaginable, *viz.* in mere *eating and drinking.*

3. In answer to the *Objection* I affirm, That the Peace and
Order of human Society depending upon, or rather consisting in
the Practice of moral Dutys; if you impose *any thing* on Mankind but what is moral, the Zeal to perform *that* must of course
abate Mens Zeal in the Practice of moral Dutys, and consequently prejudice the Peace of Society.

(1.) For, extending of *Zeal* to other Objects besides Morality,
must take off a Portion of our Zeal for the Practice of Morality.

(2.) Since Mankind can never be perfect in the performance
of their Duty, they will ever chuse to be punctual in that which
is easiest to be done: and therefore if you impose any Speculations on Men, they will not fail in their *Zeal* for them, and
leave a proportionable share of Morality undone.

(3.) It is matter of daily experience, that *Zeal* for imposing
Speculations does destroy the Practice of Morality; and every
Religious Sect gives us a proof of it. For is it not obvious, that
if you contend earnestly for the Doctrines of your Sect, and
against the Doctrines of all other Sects; and in particular, if you
are zealous for the Independent Power of the Priest, his sole
Right to preach, and his Power to damn or save at his pleasure:
you shall be so far indulg'd in Vice and Wickedness, as to have
it conceal'd if possible, and if made publick, to have it colour'd
over with the most charitable Construction imaginable? Whereas,
if you are against *Predestination* in *Scotland,* or *Transubstantiation* in *France,* or against the Power of the Priest in either
Country, you shall be represented as the most infamous Wretch
(tho they have no particular Immorality to charge upon you)
and all your innocent or virtuous Actions shall be construed
after the most uncharitable manner.

Further, Are not the Streets of the City of *London* (like those
of *Rome, Paris,* or *Venice*) full of common Whores, who are in
effect publickly tolerated in their Wickedness? And are not the
Men who have dealings with them free from all Punishment, and
almost from Censure? And yet few or no Complaints are made,
of this Wickedness in the open streets, either from the *Pulpit* or

the *Press*. But if any man asserts *that a Layman may sprinkle Water in a Child's Face,* or make a Discourse in publick upon a Text of Scripture; the Press rings with the Crime, and Dr. SACHEVEREL cries out from the Pulpit,* *That the* English *Fanatick, who sets up Lay-Elders, is the greatest Monster upon earth.*

Besides, they who have an interest to enlarge their Sect and keep it united, know that nothing *tends so much to its Increase and Union,* as the Toleration of Vice and Wickedness to as great a degree as they can conveniently: for by that means they are sure to engage all the *Rogues* and *Vicious* (and by consequence the *Fools,* who will ever be led by them) in their Party. And therefore wherever the Power of the Priest is at the height, they proceed so far in the encouragement of Wickedness, as to make all Churches *Sanctuarys,* or *Places of Protection.* Pope PIUS V. confess'd this *Secret* of *supporting a Church,* when, upon hearing that the Protestants were in earnest against *Adultery* and *Fornication,* he said, *If they will not allow of such kind of sport in their Religion, it will never be of any long duration.* And this *Secret* was early put in practice with success; for ZOZIMUS tells us, *That* CONSTANTINE *the Great, after he had committed such horrible Villanys which the* Pagan *Priests told him were not to be expiated in their Religion, being assur'd by an* Egyptian . . . *that there was no Villany so great, but was to be expiated by the Sacraments of the Christian Religion, embrac'd the new Impiety* (so ZOZIMUS impiously calls the Christian Religion) *and quitted the Religion of his Ancestors.* And this Conversion of the Emperor CONSTANTINE gave occasion to JULIAN to satyrize thus our Holy Religion: *Whoever,* says he, *is guilty of Rapes, Murders, Sacrilege, or any other abominable Crime; let him be wash'd with Water, and he will become pure and holy: and if he relapses into the same Impiety, he will again become pure and holy, by thumping his Breast and beating his Head.*

6thly. It is objected, *That Free-Thinkers themselves are the most infamous, wicked, and senseless of all Mankind.*

This Objection of Wickedness and Ignorance is made by all Sects one against another, and serves to keep the several Herds and Folds of Men united together, and against one another. And

* Assize-Sermon at *Oxford,* Anno 1704.

tho in reality Men of all Sects are much alike as to Sense, where
Literature equally prevails, and every where the same as to their
Lives and Conversations (as is obvious to any indifferent Person) yet thro such Spectacles do Men see the Defects of others,
so partial are they to themselves, so ready to believe ill Reports
of those with whom they have any difference in Opinion, and to
believe good of those with whom they agree in Opinion; so apt
to put an ill Construction on any Actions of the former, and a
good one on any Actions of the latter; that nothing but the most
familiar Intercourse imaginable can make Men, who are govern'd by one sort of Priests, think they are like those in Understanding and Morals who are govern'd by another sort. But this
Objection, as it is urg'd against *Free-Thinkers,* is still with more
difficulty to be remov'd by them; because they who have Leisure,
Application, Ability and Courage to *think freely,* are so few in
number in respect of any other Sect, that they must be less able
by Conversation in the World to answer an Objection against
themselves, so early planted in Mens Minds, and so carefully
cultivated. However, I think it may be much easier answer'd
upon *Paper,* and may by shown to be more unjustly urg'd against
Free-Thinkers, than against any other sort of Men whatsoever.
In answer to it therefore, I observe,

1. That Men who use their Understandings, must have more
Sense than they who use them not; and this I take to be self-
evident. And as to the other part of the Objection, I assert, That
Free-Thinkers must, as such, be the most virtuous Persons every
where.

(1.) Because if any Man presumes to think for himself, and
in consequence of that departs from the Sentiments of the Herd
of Mankind among whom he lives, he is sure to draw upon himself the whole Malice of the Priest, and of all who believe in
him, or who hope to make their Fortune by pretending to believe in him (which must of course by 999 of 1000) and can
have no Credit but what his *Virtue,* in spite of his Enemys,
necessarily procures for him. Whereas any *profligate Fellow* is
sure of Credit, Countenance and Support, in any Sect or Party
whatsoever, tho he has no other quality to recommend him than
the worst of all Vices, *a blind Zeal to his Sect or Party.* The
Free-Thinker therefore is for his own sake in this World oblig'd

to be *virtuous* and honest; but the *Bigot* is under no such Obligation; and besides, has the temptation to become a Knave, because so many *weak People* of all *Partys* are ready to put their confidence in him purely for his *Bigotry*.

(2.) Because whoever applies himself to any Action, much more to *Free-Thinking* (which requires great Diligence and Application of Mind) must by that Habit expel all those vicious Dispositions and Passions, by which every Man out of action is toss'd and govern'd.

(3.) Besides, by much *Thinking* only, are Men able to comprehend in their minds the whole compass of human Life, and thereby to demonstrate to themselves, that Misery and Unhappiness attend the Practice of Vice, and Pleasure and Happiness the Practice of Virtue, in this Life; and that to live *pleasantly,* they must live *virtuously. For who,* says CICERO, *lives pleasantly, except him who delights in his Duty, and has well consider'd and settled his manner of Life; and who obeys the Laws not out of* Fear, *but observes and regards them because he judges it the best thing he can do?* Whereas we see by experience, that most Men, for want of considering the whole compass of human Life, mistake their own Happiness, and think it wholly consists in gratifying their present Passions and Inclinations: And accordingly are very little mov'd *even* by their Belief of future Happiness and Misery to become *virtuous,* while they are under such a mistake. And thus of course all *unthinking People* are *vicious,* unless they are prevented by some *natural Defect* or *Impediment,* or are *moral* by the Goodness of their natural Temper. CICERO admirably describes the Effects of this wrong Judgment about the Rule of Morality. Says he, *Whoever places Happiness in any thing besides Virtue, and judges of Happiness by his* present *Interest and Advantage, and not by the Rules of Honesty,* or what is good upon the whole; *if he be consistent with himself, and is not carry'd away with his own good natural Disposition, can neither be friendly, nor equitable, nor generous. No man can be courageous, who takes Pain to be the greatest Evil; nor be moderate in the enjoyment of Pleasure, who takes that to be the greatest Good.*

Christianity as Old as the Creation*

Matthew Tindal

Matthew Tindal, unlike some of his brethren, was a respectable man; as a fellow of All Souls at Oxford, he led a quiet life, and his main work, Christianity as Old as the Creation, *published in 1730, appeared when the author was past seventy.*

Christianity as Old as the Creation is what has been called "constructive deism" at its best. Relatively moderate in tone and extremely shrewd in argumentation, it appropriated what was most persuasive in liberal Christianity, and left the supernatural component of that Christianity behind. Miracles and revelations, to the extent that they are authentic, merely confirm what God has revealed to the reason. The only true religion is natural religion, that is, a religion that acknowledges the fatherhood of God and the moral law of the universe.

But, like all constructive deists, Tindal also had his critical side, and his sarcasms at the expense of the Jews and of credulous Christians (as Sir Leslie Stephen justly observed long ago) anticipate the witticisms of Voltaire.

That the Religion of Nature consists in observing those Things, which our Reason, by considering the Nature of God and Man, and the Relation we stand in to him and one another, demonstrates to be our Duty; and that those Things are plain; and likewise What they are.

B. That we may the better know whether the *Law,* or *Religion of Nature* is universal, and the Gospel a Republication of it, and not a new Religion; I desire you will give a Definition of the *Religion of Nature.*

A. By *Natural Religion,* I understand the Belief of the Existence of a God, and the Sense and Practice of those Duties which

* The excerpts that follow have been taken from *Christianity as Old as the Creation* (ed. 1732), pp. 11-27, 157-169.

result from the Knowledge we, by our Reason, have of him and his Perfections; and of ourselves, and our own Imperfections; and of the relation we stand in to him and our Fellow-Creatures; so that the *Religion of Nature* takes in every thing that is founded on the Reason and Nature of things. . . .

I suppose you will allow, that 'tis evident by the *Light of Nature,* that there is a God; or in other words, a Being absolutely perfect, and infinitely happy in himself, who is the Source of all other Beings; and that what Perfections soever the Creatures have, they are wholly deriv'd from him.

B. This, no doubt, has been demonstrated over and over; and I must own, that I can't be more certain of my own Existence, than of the Existence of such a Being.

A. Since then it is demonstrable there is such a Being, it is equally demonstrable, that the Creatures can neither add to, or take from the Happiness of that Being; and that he could have no Motive in framing his Creatures, or in giving Laws to such of them as he made capable of knowing his Will, but their own Good.

To imagine he created them at first for his own sake, and has since required things of them for that Reason, is to suppose he was not perfectly happy in himself before the Creation; and that the Creatures, by either observing, or not observing the Rules prescrib'd them, cou'd add to, or take from his Happiness.

If then a Being infinitely happy in himself, cou'd not command his Creatures any thing for his own Good; nor an all-wise Being things to no end or purpose; nor an all-good Being any thing but for their good: It unavoidably follows, nothing can be a part of the divine Law, but what tends to promote the common Interest, and mutual Happiness of his rational Creatures; and every thing that does so, must be a part of it.

As God can require nothing of us, but what makes for our Happiness; so he, who can't envy us any Happiness our Nature is capable of, can forbid us those Things only, which tend to our Hurt; and this we are as certain of, as that there is a God infinitely happy in himself, infinitely good and wise; and as God can design nothing by his Laws but our Good, so by being infinitely powerful, he can bring every thing to pass which he designs for that End.

From the Consideration of these Perfections, we cannot but have the highest Veneration, nay, the greatest Adoration and Love for this supreme Being; who, that we may not fail to be as happy as possible for such Creatures to be, has made our acting for our *present,* to be the only Means of obtaining our *future* Happiness; so that we can't sin against him, but by acting against ourselves, *i.e.* our reasonable Natures: These Reflections, which occur to every one who in the least considers, must give us a wonderful and surprizing Sense of the divine Goodness, fill us with Admiration, Transport and Extasy; (of which we daily see among contemplative Persons remarkable Instances): And not only force us to express a never-failing Gratitude in Raptures of the highest Praise and Thanksgiving; but make us strive to imitate him in our extensive Love to our Fellow-Creatures: And thus copying after the Divine Original, and taking God himself for our Precedent, must conform us to his Image, who is all Perfection and all Happiness; and who must have an inexhaustible Love for all, who thus endeavour to imitate him. . . .

The difference between the supreme Being, infinitely happy in himself, and the Creatures who are not so, is, That all his Actions, in relation to his Creatures, flow from a pure disinterested Love: whereas the Spring of all the Actions of the Creatures is their own Good: *We love God, because he first loved us* [1 John 4. 19]; and consequently, our Love to him will be in proportion to our Sense of his Goodness to us. Nor can we in the least vary from those Sentiments, which the Consideration of the divine Attributes implant in us, but we must in proportion take off from the Goodness of God, and from those Motives we have to love him as we ought.

Our Reason, which gives us a Demonstration of the divine Perfections, affords us the same concerning the Nature of those Duties God requires; not only with relation to himself, but to ourselves, and one another: These we can't but see, if we look into ourselves, consider our own Natures, and the Circumstances God has placed us in with relation to our Fellow-Creatures, and what conduces to our mutual Happiness: Our Senses, our Reason, the Experience of others as well as our own, can't fail to give us sufficient Information.

With relation to ourselves, we can't but know how we are to

act; if we consider, that God has endow'd Man with such a Nature, as makes him necessarily desire his own Good; and, therefore, he may be sure, that God, who has bestow'd this Nature on him, could not require any thing of him in prejudice of it; but, on the contrary, that he should do every thing which tends to promote the Good of it. The Health of the Body, and the Vigor of the Mind, being highly conducing to our Good, we must be sensible we offend our Maker, if we indulge our Senses to the prejudice of these: And because not only all ir-regular Passions, all unfriendly Affections carry their own Tor-ment with them, and endless Inconveniences attend the Excess of sensual Delights; and all immoderate Desires (human Nature being able to bear but a certain Proportion) disorder both Mind and Body; we can't but know we ought to use great Modera-tion with relation to our Passions, or in other Words, govern all our Actions by Reason; That, and our true Interest being in-separable. And, in a word, whoever so regulates his natural Appetites, as will conduce most to the Exercise of his Reason, the Health of his Body, and the Pleasure of his Senses, taken and consider'd together, (since herein his Happiness consists) may be certain he can never offend his Maker; who, as he governs all things according to their Natures, can't but expect his rational Creatures should act according to their Natures.

As to what God expects from Man with relation to each other; every one must know his Duty, who considers that the common Parent of Mankind has the whole Species alike under his Pro-tection, and will equally punish him for injuring others, as he would others for injuring him; and consequently, that it is his Duty to deal with them, as he expects they should deal with him in the like Circumstances. How much this is his Duty, every one must perceive, who considers himself as a weak Creature, not able to subsist without the Assistance of others, who have it in their Power to retaliate the Usage he gives them: And that he may expect, if he breaks those Rules which are necessary for Men's mutual Happiness, to be treated like a common Enemy, not only by the Persons injur'd, but by all others; who, by the common Ties of Nature, are obliged to defend and assist each other. And not only a Man's own particular Interest, but that of his Children, his Family, and all that's dear to him, obliges him to promote the common Happiness, and to endeavour to convey the fame to Posterity. . . .

In short, considering the variety of Circumstances Men are under, and these continually changing, as well as being for the most part unforeseen; 'tis impossible to have Rules laid down by any *External* Revelation for every particular Case; and therefore, there must be some standing Rule, discoverable by the *Light of Nature,* to direct us in all such Cases. And we can't be more certain, that 'tis the Will of God, that those Effects which flow from natural Causes should so flow; than we are, that 'tis the Will of God, that Men should observe, whatever the Nature of Things, and the Relation they have to one another, make fit to be observ'd; or in other Words, we can't but know, if we in the least consider, that, whatever Circumstances Men are plac'd in, by the universal Cause of all things; that 'tis his eternal and immutable Will, by his placing them in these Circumstances, that they act as these require. 'Tis absurd to imagine we are oblig'd to act thus in some Cases, and not in others; when the reason for acting thus in all is the same. This Confideration alone will direct a Man how to act in all Conditions of Life, whether *Father, Son, Husband, Servant, Subject, Master, King,* &c. Thus we see how the reason of things, or the relation they have to each other, teaches us our Duty in all cases whatever. And I may add, that the better to cause Men to observe those Rules, which make for their mutual Benefit, infinite Goodness has sown in their Hearts Seeds of Pity, Humanity and Tenderness, which, without much difficulty, cannot be eradicated; but nothing operates more strongly than that Desire Men have of being in Esteem, Credit, and Reputation with their Fellow-Creatures, not to be obtain'd without acting on the Principles of natural Justice, Equity, Benevolence, &c.

In a word, as a most beneficent Disposition in the supreme Being is the Source of all his Actions in relation to his Creatures; so he has implanted in Man, whom he has made after his own Image, a Love for his Species; the gratifying of which, in doing Acts of Benevolence, Compassion, and Good Will, produces a Pleasure that never satiates; as on the contrary, Actions of Ill-Nature, Envy, Malice, &c. never fail to produce Shame, Confusion, and everlasting Self-reproach.

And now let any one say, how 'tis possible God could more fully make known his Will to all intelligent Creatures, than by making every thing within, and without them a Declaration of it, and an Argument for observing it.

Having thus discovered our Duty, we may be sure it will always be the same; since Inconstancy, as it argues a Defect either of Wisdom or Power, can't belong to a Being infinitely wise and powerful: What unerring Wisdom has once instituted, can have no Defects; and as God is intirely free from all Partiality, his Laws must alike extend to all Times and Places.

From these Premises, I think, we may boldly draw this Conclusion, That if Religion consists in the Practice of those Duties, that result from the Relation we stand in to God and Man, our Religion must always be the same. If God is unchangeable, our Duty to him must be so too; if Human Nature continues the same, and Men at all Times stand in the same Relation to one another, the Duties which result from thence too, must always be the same: And consequently our Duty both to God and Man must, from the Beginning of the World to the End, remain unalterable; be always alike plain and perspicuous; neither chang'd in Whole, or Part: which demonstrates that no Person, if he comes from God, can teach us any other Religion, or give us any Precepts, but what are founded on those Relations. *Heaven and Earth shall sooner pass away*, than *one Tittle of this* Eternal *Law shall either be abrogated, or alter'd.*

That the Perfection and Happiness of all rational Beings, supreme as well as subordinate, consists in living up to the Dictates of their Nature.

To make This (since all our Happiness depends on it), if possible, more plain: The Principle from which all human Actions flow, is the Desire of Happiness; and God, who does nothing in vain, would in vain have implanted this Principle, This only innate Principle in Mankind, if he had not given them Reason to discern what Actions make for, and against their Happiness.

B. Wherein do you take the Happiness of rational Creatures to consist? Without knowing That, this Controversy can't be determin'd; and when 'tis known, our Dispute must soon be ended.

A. The Happiness of all Beings whatever, consists in the Perfections of their Nature; and the Nature of a rational Being is most perfect, when it is perfectly rational; that is, when it governs all its Actions by the Rules of right Reason; for then it arrives at the most perfect, and consequently the happiest State a rational Nature can aspire to: and every Deviation from the Rules of Right Reason, being an Imperfection, must carry with it a proportionable Unhappiness; and a Man's Happiness and Duty must consist in the same things, since no One can be oblig'd to do any thing that does not some way or other contribute to his Happiness; and consequently, according to the Sense Men have of their own Happiness, and of the Means which will naturally procure it, they may assuredly attain the Knowledge of their respective Duties.

B. If we know wherein the Happiness of God, who is necessarily happy, consists, we might judge wherein consists the Happiness of Man made after God's own Image; and whether Happiness, or Misery, are the necessary Consequence of his Actions. . . .

If the Perfection, and consequently the Happiness of God, consists in the Purity and Rectitude of his Nature, we, as far as we can arrive to a like Purity and Rectitude, must be so far necessarily happy; since by living according to the Rules of Right Reason, we more and more implant in us the moral Perfections of God, from which his Happiness is inseparable. We then, if I may so say, *live the Life of God;* that is, we, in our Place and Station, live after the same manner, and by the same Rules as he does in his; and we do what God himself would do was he in our place; and there would be no other difference between his Life and ours, but what arises from our different States and Relations; since the same Rules would determine our Wills as determine his Will; and by our repeated Acts of Virtue, we should be continually making nearer and nearer Approaches to the most perfect, and the most happy Being. By this Conduct, we, as the Scriptures assure us, shou'd be made Partakers of the *Divine Nature, be born of God,* and *be perfect as our heavenly Father is perfect;* and can that be without being as happy as we are perfect? Hence we may contemplate the great Dignity of our *Rational* Nature, since our Reason for Kind, tho' not for Degree, is of the same Nature with that of God's; nay, 'tis our Reason which makes us the Image of God himself, and is the common Bond which unites Heaven and Earth; the Creatures, and the Creator; and if our Happiness is limited, 'tis because our Reason is so: 'Tis God alone, who has an unlimited Reason and Happiness. . . .

I think, we may conclude, that Men, according as they do, or do not partake of the Nature of God, must unavoidably be either happy, or miserable: And herein appears the great Wisdom of God, in making Mens Misery and Happiness the necessary and inseparable Consequence of their Actions; and that rational Actions carry with them their own Reward, and irrational their own Punishment: This, I think, can't be deny'd, as long as there are some Actions naturally beneficial to us, and others as hurtful; and that there's no Virtue, but what has some Good inseparably annex'd to it; and no Vice, but what as necessarily carries with it some Evil: and if our rational Nature is to be the same in the next Life, as it is in this, our Actions must produce Effects of the same Kind and that too in a much higher degree.

In this Life, 'tis true, we can't be perfectly happy; as subject to Diseases and Disasters: We are imperfect ourselves and have none to converse with but imperfect Creatures; and yet if we act according to the Dictates of Right Reason, we shall receive, even here, true inward Comfort and Satisfaction; and hereafter, when we are freed from those Imperfections, compleat Happiness: On the contrary, the Man who abandons his Reason, besides the Misery of all sorts an irrational Conduct will bring on him, must feel in his Mind, Pain and Anguish even in this Life; and in the Life to come, when there are no sensual things to divert his Thoughts, insupportable Grief and Misery.

Tho' human Law-givers are forced to have recourse to Punishments, which are not connected with the things they forbid; yet a Being of infinite Power is not thus straiten'd, but may make one the necessary Consequence of the other: And, indeed, how can it be otherwise, since Good and Evil have their Foundation in the essential Difference of Things, and their Nature is fix'd and immoveable: And consequently, our Happiness depends on the intrinsick Nature of the one, and our Misery on the intrinsick Nature of the other.

As God, whose infinite Wisdom sets him above being deceiv'd, or influenc'd by any wrong Affections, acts in constant Conformity to the Reason and Nature of Things; and 'tis a Contradiction to his Nature for him to do any thing that is not fit and reasonable; so he would have fram'd our Nature in contradiction to his own, if he had oblig'd us to act otherwise. No, God can never give us Commands repugnant to his own Nature, or require us to do what he himself abhors to do. The End for which God has given us Reason, is to compare Things, and the Relation they stand in to each other; and from thence to judge of the Fitness and Unfitness of Actions; and could not our Reason judge soundly in all such Matters, it could not have answer'd the End for which infinite Wisdom and Goodness bestow'd that excellent Gift; and for which we can't enough adore the Goodness of God.

Had God, from time to time, spoke to all Mankind in their several Languages, and his Words had miraculously convey'd the same Ideas to all Persons; yet he could not speak more plainly than he has done by the Things themselves, and the Relation which Reason shews there is between them: Nay, since 'tis impossible in any Book, or Books, that a particular Rule cou'd be given for every Case, we must even then have had recourse to the Light of Nature to teach us our Duty in most Cases, especially considering the numberless Circumstances which attend us, and which, perpetually varying, may make the same Actions, according as Men are differently affected by them, either good or bad. And I may add, that most of the particular Rules laid down in the Gospel for our Direction, are spoken after such a figurative Manner, that except we judge of their Meaning, not merely by the Letter, but by what the Law of Nature antecedently declares to be our Duty, they are apt to lead us wrong. . . .

Tho' the Relation we stand in to God, is not artificial as most are amongst Men, who want each other's Assistance; but is natural at least on our part; yet this does not hinder, but that we may know by Reason, the End he had in being related to us as Creator and Governour; and what he requires of his Creatures and Subjects: This the divine Nature, which contains in itself all Perfection, and all Happiness, plainly points out to us. And if

we are once certain of the End of God's entring into this Relation with Man, we may be as certain from his Wisdom and Goodness, and all his divine Perfections, that he will require no more
of us than the End he had in entring into this Relation requires.

If it would be unjust and tyrannical in an earthly Governour,
to exact Things of his Subjects, that do not contribute to the End
for which this Relation between them was enter'd into; can we
suppose a Governour of infinite Wisdom and Goodness, who
has always in his mind the End for which he governs Mankind,
will act the Tyrant, and put them under severe Penalties for not
observing such things as have no relation to the End for which
he created, and governs them?

There's no Relation among Men without a mutual Obligation
arising from it; Parents owe a Duty to Children as well as
Children to Parents; but are not we in a stricter Sense, the Children of God, and Parents only Instruments in his hands? since
'tis God, who from Nothing brings us into Being, frames us after
the Manner that best pleases him, imprints on us what Faculties,
Inclinations, Desires and Passions he thinks fit: And is not God
from his innate Goodness and Equity, under a Obligation to
treat us more kindly than earthly Parents do their best-beloved
Children, who beget them without designing it? Whereas God,
whose Actions are govern'd by infinite Goodness, could have no
Motive to bring us into Being (which of itself is no Blessing) but
our Good; and for the same reason preserves us in Being: nor
can so kind and tender a Parent play the Tyrant, and impose
Commands on us, which do not flow from the Relations we stand
in to him, and to one another. . . .

In short, if the Relations between Things, and the Fitness resulting from thence, be not the sole Rule of God's Actions, must
not God be an arbitrary Being? and then what a miserable Condition will Mankind be in! Since an arbitrary Will might change
every Moment, and those Things which entitled Men to God's
Favour to-day, might make them incur his Displeasure to-mor-
row: Nay, he might at the same time have a secret Will opposite
to his reveal'd Will; or have different Will for every different
Person; or might reveal his arbitrary Commands so obscurely,
as to cause the utmost Confusion; but if God only commands
what the Nature of Things shew to be fit, 'tis scarce possible,

that Men (tho' now endlessly divided upon the account of their different Traditions) should mistake their Duty; since a Mind that's attentive can as easily distinguish *fit* from *unfit,* as the Eye can Beauty from Deformity, or the Ear Harmony from Discord: And if no Commands can alter the Nature of Things, or make that *fit* which is in itself *unfit,* external Revelation must attend the Nature and Relation of Things, and can only speak what those speak. As for instance, 'tis not in our power, tho' ever so often commanded, to love the Deity, while we conceive him an arbitrary Being acting out of Humour and Caprice; nor could any Commands, supposing such possible, oblige us not to love him, while we believe him a kind and beneficent Being; so that as long as we have right Notions of God, we can't but love, and adore him as we ought.

Thus, I think, I have fully prov'd from the Nature of God and Man, and the Relations we stand in to him and one another, that the divine Precepts can't vary; and that these Relations, which are the permanent Voice of God, by which he speaks to all Mankind, do at all times infallibly point out to us our Duty in all the various Circumstances of Life. . . .

That they, who, to magnify Revelation, weaken the Force of the Religion of Reason and Nature, strike at all Religion; and that there can't be two independent Rules for the Government of human Actions.

B. In my Opinion you lay too great a Stress on fallible Reason, and too little on infallible Revelation; and therefore I must needs say, your arguing wholly from Reason would make some of less Candour than myself, take you for an errant *Free-thinker.*

A. Whatever is true by Reason, can never be false by Revelation; and if God can't be deceiv'd himself, or be willing to deceive Men, the Light he hath given to distinguish between religious Truth and Falshood, cannot, if duly attended to, deceive them in things of so great Moment.

They who do not allow Reason to judge in Matters of Opinion or Speculation, are guilty of as great Absurdity as the *Papists,* who will not allow the Senses to be Judges in the Case of *Transubstantiation,* tho' a Matter directly under their Cognizance;

nay, the Absurdity, I think, is greater in the first Case, because Reason is to judge whether our Senses are deceiv'd: And if no Texts ought to be admitted as a Proof in a matter contrary to Sense, they ought certainly as little to be admitted in any Point contrary to Reason.

In a word, to suppose any thing in Revelation inconsistent with Reason, and, at the same time, pretend it to be the Will of God, is not only to destroy that Proof, on which we conclude it to be the Will of God, but even the Proof of the Being of a God; since if our reasoning Faculties duly attended to deceive us, we can't be sure of the Truth of any one Proposition; but every thing wou'd be alike uncertain, and we should for ever fluctuate in a State of universal Scepticism: Which shews how absurdly they act, who, on pretence of magnifying Tradition, endeavour to weaken the Force of Reason, (tho' to be sure they always except their own;) and thereby foolishly sap the Foundation, to support the Superstructure; but as long as Reason is against Men, they will be against Reason. We must not, therefore, be surpriz'd, to see some endeavour to reason Men out of their Reason; tho' the very Attempt to destroy Reason by Reason, is a Demonstration Men have nothing but Reason to trust to.

And to suppose any thing can be true by Revelation, which is false by Reason, is not to support that thing, but to undermine Revelation; because nothing unreasonable, nay, what is not highly reasonable, can come from a God of unlimited, universal, and eternal Reason. As evident as this Truth is, yet that shall not hinder me from examining in a proper Place, whatever you can urge from Revelation. And give me leave to add, that I shall not be surpris'd, if for so laudable an Attempt, as reconciling Reason and Revelation, which have been so long set at variance, I should be censur'd as a *Free-thinker;* a Title, that, however invidious it may seem, I am far from being asham'd of; since one may as well suppose a Man can reason without thinking at all, as reason well without thinking freely. But,

The irreconcileable Enemies of Reason seeing it too gross, in this reasoning Age, to attack Reason openly, do it covertly under the Name of *Free-thinking;* not despairing, but that the time may come again, when the Laity shall stifle every Thought rising in their Minds, tho' with ever so much Appearance of Truth, as a Suggestion of Satan, if it clashes with the real, or pretended Opinions of their Priests.

B. Tho' you talk so much about Reason, you have not defin'd what you mean by that Word.

A. When we attribute any Operation to it, as distinguishing between Truth and Falshood, &c. we mean by it the rational Faculties; but when we ascribe no such Operation to it, as when we give a *Reason* for a thing, &c. we then understand by it, any Medium, by which our rational Faculties judge of the Agreement, or Disagreement of the Terms of any Proposition; and if an Author writes intelligibly, we may easily discern in which of these two Senses he takes the Word. But to go to the Bottom of this Matter;

It will be requisite to give a more distinct Account of *Reason* in both these Senses. By the rational Faculties then, we mean the natural Ability a Man has to *apprehend, judge,* and *infer:* The *immediate Objects* of which Faculties are, not the things themselves, but the *Ideas* the Mind conceives of them. While our *Ideas* remain single, they fall under the *Apprehension,* and are express'd by *simple Terms;* when join'd, under the *Judgment,* and express'd by *Propositions;* when so join'd as to need the *Intervention* of some other *Idea* to compare 'em with, in order to form a *Judgment,* they become by that *Intervention,* the Subject of *Inference,* or *Argumentation;* and this is term'd, *Syllogism* or *Argument.* It must be observ'd too, that all the *Ideas* we have, or can have, are either by *Sensation* or *Reflection;* by the first, we have our *Ideas* of what passes, or exists without; by the second, of what passes, or exists within the Mind: And in the View, or Contemplation of these consists all our Knowledge; that being nothing but *the Perception of the Agreement,* or *Disagreement of our Ideas.* And any two of these, when join'd together, so as to be affirm'd or deny'd of each other, make what we call a *Proposition;* when consider'd apart, what we call the *Terms* of that *Proposition;* the *Agreement,* or *Disagreement* of which *Terms* being express'd by the rightly affirming, or denying 'em of each other, is what we call *Truth;* the Perception of their Agreement or Disagreement, is what we term *Knowledge:* This

Knowledge accrues either immediately on the bare Intuition of these two *Ideas,* or *Terms* so join'd, and is therefore styl'd *Intuitive Knowledge;* or self-evident *Truth:* Or by the Intervention of some other Idea, or Ideas, as a common Measure for the other two; and is therefore call'd the *Medium,* by which Reason judges of their Agreement or Disagreement; and this is call'd *Demonstrative Knowledge,* which is never to be had without the help of the other. For,

If there were not some Propositions which need not to be prov'd, it would be in vain for Men to argue with one another; because they then could bring no Proofs but what needed to be prov'd.— Those Propositions which need no Proof, we call self-evident; because by comparing the Ideas, signify'd by the Terms of such Propositions, we immediately discern their Agreement, or Disagreement: This is, as I said before, what we call intuitive Knowledge, and is the Knowledge of God himself, who sees all things by Intuition; and may, I think, be call'd *divine Inspiration;* as being immediately from God, and not acquir'd by any human Deduction, or drawing of Consequences: This, certainly, is that divine, that uniform Light, which shines in the Minds of all Men, and enables them to discern whatever they do discern; since without it there could be no Demonstration, no Knowledge, but invincible Obscurity, and universal Uncertainty.

Where a Proposition can't be made evident, by comparing the two Ideas or Terms of it with each other, it is render'd so by intermediate Ideas or Terms; whereby the Agreement, or Disagreement of the Ideas under Examination, or the Truth of that Proposition is perceiv'd; and when there is an intuitive Perception of the Agreement, or Disagreement of the intermediate Ideas in each Step of the Progression, then, and not till then, it becomes demonstrative Knowledge; otherwise it can rise no higher than Probability, which consists not in a certain, but a likely Connexion between the Terms of a Proposition, and the intermediate Proofs of it: So that every Proposition that's only probable, must have a proportionable Degree of Uncertainty, otherwise it would amount to Demonstration; and consequently, Probability, as well as Certainty, is founded on the

Relation it has to self-evident Truths; because where no Relation to them of *any Sort* can be discover'd, there is no room for Certainty, or Probability.

Hence we see that all wrong Reasoning is the Effect of Rashness, and consists either in taking Propositions to have a certain Connexion with self-evident Truths, when they have but a probable one; or imagining there's a probable Connexion, when there's no Connexion at all; or else mistaking the Degrees of Probability.

B. The *Quakers* are very positive, that there is in all Mankind, a Principle of Action distinct from Reason, (and which is not Inspiration) by which all are to be govern'd in Matters of Religion, as they are by Reason in other Matters; and which they commonly call *the Light within.*

A. Was there any such Principle, Men destitute of all Reason were as capable of knowing all Matters of Religion, as if they had been ever so rational. 'Tis strange, that all Mankind should have a Principle of acting, of which they never were sensible; nor can these modern Discoveries tell them what it is, or how it operates; nor do they themselves ever use it in any of their Debates about Religion; but argue like other Men from Principles that are in common to all Mankind, and prove Propositions that are not self-evident by those that are so; and confute false and bad Reasons (of which they can only judge by Reason) by true and good Reasons; which supposes that Reason, however fallible it may be, is all rational Creatures have to trust to; and that 'tis the highest Commendation of Religion; that it is a *reasonable Service.* And since this is an Age, where Words without Meaning, or Distinctions without Difference, will not pass current; why should they, who otherwise appear to have good Sense, thus impose on themselves, and be expos'd to others, for such senseless Notions, as can only serve to prejudice People against their other rational Principles? But 'tis the Fate of most Sects to be fondest of their ugliest Brats. But not to deviate,

Were it not for those self-evident Notions, which are the Foundation of all our Reasonings, there could be no intellectual Communication between God and Man; nor, as we are fram'd, can God ascertain us of any Truth, but by shewing its Agreement with those self-evident Notions, which are the Tests by which we are to judge of every thing, even the Being of a God, and Natural Religion; which, tho' not knowable by Intuition, are to be demonstrated by such Proofs, which have, mediately or immediately, a necessary Connexion with our self-evident Notions. And therefore to weaken the Force of Demonstration, is to strike at all Religion, and even the Being of God; and not to give Probability its due Weight, is to strike at the Authority of that Revelation you contend for; because, that God reveal'd his Will by *Visions, Dreams, Trances,* or any other Way besides the Light of Nature, can only come under the Head of Probability. And,

If it be but probable, that God made any external Revelation at all, it can be but probable, tho' perhaps, not in the same Degree of Probability, that he made this, or that Revelation: And this Evidence all pretend to, since, perhaps, there never was a Time or Place, where some external Revelation was not believ'd, and its Votaries equally confident, that Theirs was a true Revelation: And, indeed, the prodigious Numbers of Revelations, which from time to time have been in the World, shew how easily Mankind may in this Point be impos'd on. And as there can be no Demonstration of the Revelation itself, so neither can there be any of its Conveyance to Posterity; much less that this, or that, has been convey'd intire to distant times and Places; especially, if the Revelation be of any Bulk; and which may have gone through the Hands of Men, who, not only in the dark Ages of the Church, but even in the Beginning, if we judge by the Number of corrupted Passages, and even forg'd Books, were capable of any pious Fraud. . . .

B. I don't think we ought to have the same Regard for Reason as Men had formerly; when That was the sole Rule God had given them for the Government of their Actions; since now we Christians have two supreme, independent Rules, *Reason* and *Revelation;* and both require an absolute Obedience.

A. I can't see how that is possible; for if you are to be govern'd by the latter, That supposes you must take every thing on Trust; or merely because it's said by those, for whose Dictates You are to have an implicit Faith: For to examine into the Truth of what they say, is renouncing their Authority; as on

the contrary, if Men are to be govern'd by their Reason, they
are not to admit any thing farther than as they see it reasonable.
To suppose both consistent, is to suppose it consistent to take,
and not to take, things on trust.

To receive Religion on the account of Authority supposes,
that if the Authority promulgated a different Religion, we should
be oblig'd to receive it; and indeed, it's an odd Jumble, to prove
the Truth of a Book by the Truth of the Doctrines it contains,
and at the same time conclude those Doctrines to be true, because contain'd in that Book; and yet this is a Jumble every
one makes, who contends for Mens being absolutely govern'd
both by Reason and Authority.

What can be a fuller Evidence of the Sovereignty of Reason,
than that all Men, when there is any thing in their traditional
Religion, which in its literal Sense can't be defended by Reason,
have recourse to any Method of Interpretation, tho' ever so
forc'd, in order to make it appear reasonable. . . .

In a Word, when Men, in defending their own, or attacking
other traditionary Religions, have recourse to the Nature or
Reason of Things; does not That shew, they believe the Truth
of all traditionary Religions is to be try'd by it; as being That,
which must tell them what is true or false in Religion? And were
there not some Truths relating to Religion of themselves so evident, as that all must agree in them, nothing relating to Religion
could be prov'd, every thing would want a farther Proof; and if
there are such evident Truths, must not all others be try'd by
their Agreement with them? And are not these the Tests, by
which we are to distinguish the only true Religion from the
many false ones? And do not all Parties alike own, there are
such Tests drawn from the nature of Things, each crying their
Religion contains every thing worthy, and nothing unworthy
of having God for its Author; thereby cofessing that Reason
enables them to tell what is worthy of having God for its Author. And if Reason tells them this, does it not tell them every
thing that God can be suppos'd to require?

In short, nothing can be more certain, than that there are
some things in their own Nature good, some evil; and others
neither good nor evil; and for the same reason God commands
the Good, and forbids the Evil, he leaves Men at liberty in

Things indifferent; it being inconsistent with his Wisdom to reward the Observance of such things, and with his Goodness to punish for not observing them. And as he could have no End in creating Mankind, but their common Good; so they answer the End of their Creation, who do all the Good they can: And to enable Men to do this, God has given them Reason to distinguish Good from Evil, useful from useless Things: Or, in other Words, has made them moral Agents, capable of discerning the Relations they stand in to God and one another; and the Duties resulting from these Relations, so necessary to their common Good: And consequently, Religion, thus founded on these immutable Relations, must at all Times, and in all Places, be alike immutable; since external Revelation, not being able to make any Change in these Relations, and the Duties that necessarily result from them, can only recommend, and inculcate these Duties; except we suppose, that God at last acted the Tyrant, and impos'd such Commands, as the Relations we stand in to him, and one another, no ways require.

To imagine any external Revelation not to depend on the Reason of Things, is to make Things give Place to Words; and implies, that from the Time this Rule commenc'd, we are forbid to act as moral Agents, in judging what is Good or Evil; Fit or Unfit; and that we are to make no other Use of our Reason, than to see what is the literal Meaning of Texts; and to admit That only to be the Will of God, tho' ever so inconsistent with the Light of Nature, and the eternal Reason of Things. Is not this to infer, there's nothing Good or Evil in itself, but that all depends on the Will of an arbitrary Being; which, tho' it may change every Moment, is to be unalterably found in such a Book? And,

All Divines, I think, now agree in owning, that there's a Law of Reason, antecedent to any external Revelation, that God can't dispence, either with his Creatures or himself, for not observing; and that no external Revelation can be true, that in the least Circumstance, or minutest Point, is inconsistent with it. If so, how can we affirm any one thing in Revelation to be true, 'till we perceive, by that Understanding, which God hath given us to discern the Truth of things; whether it agrees with this immutable Law, or not.

If we can't believe otherwise than as things appear to our

Understandings, to suppose God requires us to give up our Understandings (a Matter we can't know but by using our Understanding) to any Authority whatever, is to suppose he requires Impossibilities. And our self-evident Notions being the Foundation of all Certainty, we can only judge of things, as they are found to be more or less agreeable to them; to deny This on any Pretence whatever, can serve only to introduce an universal Scepticism. . . .

B. Tho' Reason may be the Judge; yet the Scripture, we say, is the Rule, by which Reason must judge of the Truth of things.

A. If it be such a Rule, must it not have all the Qualifications necessary to make it so? But if Reason must tell us what those Qualifications are, and whether they are to be found in Scripture; and if one of those Qualifications is, that the Scripture must be agreeable to the Nature of things; does not that suppose the Nature of things to be the standing Rule, by which we must judge of the Truth of all those Doctrines contain'd in the Scriptures? So that the Scripture can only be a secondary Rule, as far as it is found agreeable to the Nature of things; or to those self-evident Notions, which are the Foundation of all Knowledge and Certainty.

In short, no Man can any more discern the Objects of his own Understanding, and their Relations, by the Faculties of another, than he can see with another Man's Eyes; or that one Ship can be guided by the Helm of another: And therefore, he, who demands a Man's Assent to any thing, without conveying into his Mind such Reasons as may produce a Sense of the Truth of it; erects a Tyranny over his Understanding, and demands an impossible Tribute. No Opinion, tho' ever so certain to one Man, can be infus'd into another as certain, by any Method, but by opening his Understanding, so that he may find the Reasonableness of it in his own Mind; and consequently, the only *Criterion*, by which he tries his own Reasonings, must be the internal Evidence he has already of certain Truths, and the Agreeableness of his Inferences to them. And,

To suppose a Creature to have Reason to direct him, and that he is not to be directed by it, is a Contradiction; and if we are religious as we are rational, can Religion oblige us not to be govern'd by Reason, tho' but for a Moment? Nay, what is the

Religion of all rational Beings, but what the Scripture terms it, *a reasonable Service?* Or, their Reason employ'd on such Subjects, as conduce to the Dignity of the rational Nature? So that Religion and Reason were not only given for the same End, the Good of Mankind; but they are, as far as such Subjects extend, the same, and commence together. And if God can no otherwise apply to Men, but by applying to their Reason, (which he is continually doing by the Light of Nature) does he not by that bid them use their Reason? And can God at the same time forbid it, by requiring an implicit Faith in any Person whatever.

If you allow, that Men by their reasoning Faculties are made like unto God, and fram'd after his Image; and that Reason is the most excellent Gift God can bestow; do they not destroy this Likeness, deface this Image, and give up the Dignity of human Nature, when they give up their Reason to any Person whatever?

Can we lay too great a Stress on Reason, when we consider, 'tis only by virtue of it God can hold Communication with Man? Nor can otherwise, if I may so speak, witness for himself, or assert the Wisdom and Goodness of his Conduct; than by submitting his Ways to Mens cool Deliberation, and strict Examination? since 'tis from the Marks we discern in the Laws of the Universe, and its Government, that we can demonstrate it to be govern'd by a God of infinite Wisdom and Goodness: He, whose Reason does not enable him to do This, can neither discern the Wisdom, Goodness, or even the Being of a God. . . .

A Defence of the Discourses on Miracles*

Thomas Woolston

All radical movements have their lunatic fringe, and the deist movement is no exception. Thomas Woolston was an eccentric; his virulent rhetoric exceeds all bounds even in an age used to virulent rhetoric. But he was not simply a madman; his arguments, confused and vicious as they sometimes are, had a certain persuasive power. They became extremely popular on the Continent, where they were quoted with much relish.

Woolston's Six *Discourses on the Miracles of Our Saviour were published separately from 1727 to 1729; and his* Defence *of these discourses, from which our selection is taken, came out in 1729. It was his last performance; in 1730, he was jailed and heavily fined, and in 1733, still in prison, unable to pay his fine, he died.*

Odd as his intellectual productions are, Woolston's procedure is perfectly plain: Collins had attacked the credibility of the prophecies; Woolston attacked the credibility of the miracles, on the same grounds, and with the same methods. The French deists, in particular, were to find his assault on the miraculous worth copying.

TO THE QUEEN.

Madam,

Not long since the Bishop *of St. David's presented to Your* Majesty *his* Vindication; *as I would have done this my* Defence, *if I had known how to get Access to Your Royal Presence.*

Your Majesty *will perceive, that here's a sad War broke out between the* Bishop *and my self, about* Miracles; *which, in all probability, will cost a large Effusion of Words; and, unless Your* Majesty *can accommodate the Difference, will hardly be terminated without the Slaughter of many Notions and Arguments.*

* From *A Defence of the Discourses on Miracles* (1729), pp. 1-10, 12-23, 25-29, 57-61, 69-71.

The Bishop *is for making Your* Majesty *the Arbitress of our Controversy, which I consent to; and he talks of Your singular Qualifications to preside at it, which I as certainly believe, as that a* Bishop *will not lye nor flatter.*

Had I known before of Your Majesty's *Abilities at this Controversy, I should have gone near to have applauded You for them; and the World would readily have believed my Praises of You to be just, because I had no Bishoprick nor* Translation *in View for them.*

If Your Majesty *has no extraordinary Talent at this Controversy, I trust, You are wiser than to think the better of Your self for the* Bishop's *Compliment. You'll not be vain; tho' he is fulsome.*

But the Bishop, *Madam, has done me wrong. He would insinuate, that I am disaffected to the* King's *Title and Government; which is entirely false. I Love and Honour Your whole Royal Family, and often pray for Your* Majesty *too,* without Pay, *which is more than any* Bishop *in* England *has done for You.*

And what are my Prayers for Your Majesty? *That God may prolong Your Days to the Comfort of Your Royal Progeny, and the Joy of these Nations; That the Felicity of Your Life may be uninterrupted by Enemies and Misfortunes; and That after a good old Age, when Life is no longer desirable to the happyest Princes, You may be transferr'd to an heavenly and immortal Crown of Glory. This is the hearty and voluntary Prayer of,*

Madam,

London, September 27, 1729.

> *Your Majesty's*
> *most humble,*
> *most obedient,*
> *and faithful Servant,*
> THOMAS WOOLSTON.

At last, one Volume of *Bishop Smalbroke*'s mountainous Work, that the *Press* has been so long pregnant with, is brought forth: And I don't doubt, but it answers the Expectations of the *Clergy,* who will extol it to the Skies, and applaud it to the Populace, as an absolute Confutation of my *Discourses;* but I would advise them, if it be not too late, not to be too profuse in their Commendations of it, for fear that an Occasion should be given them to blush for their want of Judgment. We have had Instances of Books before now (and one very remarkable, in the Case of *Boyle* against *Bentl*[e]*y*) that have met with a general Approbation, till they have been sifted into, and upon Examination found empty; and it is not impossible, but *this* of the *Bishop* before us, may meet with the same Fate.

I had conceived a great Opinion of this *Bishop*'s Learning and Abilities, and, if he had not sent (*a*) two simple *Harbingers* before-hand, should have been so apprehensive of his Acuteness, that nothing, but a thorough Persuasion of the Goodness of my Cause, and of my Power to defend it, could have kept me from Flight before him. But I stand my Ground, and shall, against greater Adversaries than this *Bishop,* who has more weakly and maliciously attack'd me, than cou'd have been expected from one of his reputed Candour and Learning; and given me greater Advantages to insult and triumph over him, than I could wish or desire.

Many other little *Whifflers* in Divinity have before attack'd me with their *Squibs* and *Squirts* from the *Press,* but I despised them all, as unworthy of my particular Regard and Notice, reserving my self for Defence against this *Bishop*'s grand Assault; when, by the by, I might have an Opportunity to animadvert on one or other of them. Some of these *Whifflers,* like Men of Honour, have set their Names to their Works; others very prudently have concealed their Names, which, upon the best Enquiry I could make, I have not been able to discover, or I had given them a Rebuke for their Impudence and Slanders. It may be wonder'd, that any polemical Authors, especially when they write on the orthodox and establish'd Side of the Question, should conceal themselves, and that they are not tempted with the Hopes of Reward and Applause to make themselves known. I will say what I think here, that it's never Modesty in such *anonymous* Authors (for we *Scriblers* in Divinity, whatever we may pretend, have always a good Conceit of our selves) but Apprehensions of a sharp Reply to their Dishonour. And this is

(*a*) His Sermon before the Societies for Reformation; and his Charge to the Clergy.

the true Reason, why some of my Adversaries industriously conceal themselves, knowing that they are guilty of wilful and malicious Lies and Calumnies, which I should chastise them for. But, as their Names are supprest, they know, it's to no Purpose for me to expose their Malice, because no body can be put to shame for it.

The *Bishop* of St. *David's* acts here a more glorious Part: He comes not behind me, like other *Cowards,* to give me a secret Knock on the Pate, but like a couragious Champion, looks me in the Face, and admonishes me to stand upon my Guard. This is bravely done in him! And I have no Fault to find, but that he is providing himself with *Seconds* in the Controversy, I mean the *Civil Powers,* and calling upon them to destroy me, before the Battle is well begun, and whether he gets the better of me or not. This is not fairly nor honourably done of the *Bishop,* and I have Reason to complain of it. Tho' I think my self equal, if not superior in the Dispute, to any of our *Bishops,* yet I am not a Match for the *King*'s Power, neither would I lift up my Hand, or use my Pen against him for all the World. If the *Bishop* will yield to a fair Combat, and desire the Civil Authority to stand by and see fair Play between us, I will engage with him upon any Terms. But to make the *Civil Powers* Parties in our Quarrel, and to bespeak them, right or wrong, to favour his Side, is intolerable, and what we spiritual Gladiators ought to abhor and detest.

I liked the *Bishop,* when he proposed to the *Queen* to be *Arbitress* of our Controversy. As I will not here question her Qualifications to judge in it, so the first Opportunity I have of waiting on her *Majesty,* I will join my Requests to her to accept of the Trouble and Office. After she has fix'd the Terms of Disputation, and thought of a proper Reward for the *Victor,* or a Punishment for the *Conquer'd,* then will we proceed, and either dispute the Matter from the Press, or scold it out in the Queen's Presence, as she shall think it most conducive to the Edification of herself, and of her Court-Ladies.

But the *Bishop*'s Proposal here, and Compliment on the *Queen,* is but the Copy of his Countenance. He'll submit to no Arbitration: No, no, he's for having the Civil Powers to be immediate Executioners (without further hearing what I have to say for my self) of his Wrath and Vengeance upon me. He's for having them to take it for granted, that he has proved me an *Infidel* and *Blasphemer,* and would have them to inflict some exemplary Punishment upon me, so as to incapacitate me for ever writing more. Wherefore else does he say thus? "Indeed a more proper Occasion cannot possibly happen in a Nation, where Christianity is establish'd by human *Laws,* to invigorate the Zeal of the Magistrate, in putting the Laws in Execution against so flagrant a Sort of Profaneness, that tramples with such Indignity on the Grounds of the *Christian* Faith; and to convince the World that the *Minister* of that *God,* who is so highly affronted, *bears not the Sword in vain.* And certainly the Higher Powers have great Reason to exert their Authority on this and the like Occasions."

I was astonish'd at this Passage, with some others, in the *Bishop*'s *Dedication,* and could hardly believe my Eyes when I read it; that a Scholar, a Christian, and a Protestant Bishop, should breath so much Fury and Fire for the kindling again of *Smithfield* Faggots! That any Thing of human Shape should so thirst after that Destruction of another, which would turn to the Ruin of his own Reputation and Honour! Does the *Bishop* believe that he has clearly confuted me, or does he not? If he believes, and others know that I am absolutely confuted, then there's an End of the Controversy, the Danger of my *blasphemous* Books is over; and why should I undergo any Punishment, which would move the Compassion of many, and give a greater Reputation to my Writings than they do deserve? Does the *Bishop* think he has confuted me? This is Honour and Triumph enough to him; who, of all Men, should not desire me to be otherwise punish'd, for fear of getting the Character of a merciless and implacable Conqueror. Am I in my own Opinion confuted and baffled? This would be Pain and Mortification enough, even worse than Death. For, however we polemical *Writers* may pretend a Readiness to part with our Errors upon Conviction, as if we could easily yield to our Adversaries, yet it goes to the Hearts of us to be out-done in Reason and Argument. As it is said of *Bishop Stillingfleet,* that, being sensible of his Insufficiency to contend with Mr. *Lock,* he grieved and pined away upon it: So I, upon Supposition the Bishop of St. *David's* has confuted me, must not only necessarily afflict my self, but undergo the Shame of the Reproaches of the People, for my wicked and impotent Efforts to subvert their Religion: And what would the *Bishop* have more? He could desire no more, if he had absolutely confuted me: But it's plain he dares not trust to his own Confutation of me; it's plain he's afraid of, what he is conscious may be made, a smart Reply to him, and therefore he calls upon the Civil Magistrate for his Help to prevent it.

After that the *Bishop* of *London* had publish'd his *Pastoral Letter,* and it was reported that the *Bishop* of St. *David's* was preparing a strenuous Vindication of the *litteral* Story of *Jesus's* Miracles, I concluded that the Prosecution would immediately be dropp'd, and that the Clergy were betaking themselves to that Christian, Rational, and Philosophical Course of Confutation, and would no longer make use of Persecution, which is the Armour of hot, furious, and ignorant Bigots. And there is one Passage in the *Bishop's Pastoral Letter,* which I interpreted as a Grant of full Liberty; but, whether I am apt to mistake the Sense of the Fathers of the *Primitive* Church or not, I find I did misconstrue the Words of a Father of our *English* Church, and turn'd them to another and better Purpose than he aim'd at. His Words are these "And as to the *blasphemous manner,* in which a late Writer has taken the Liberty to treat our Savior's Miracles, and the Author of them; tho' I am far from contending, that the Grounds of the Christian Religion, and the Doctrines of it, may not be discuss'd at all Times in a calm, decent, and serious Way (on the contrary, I am sure that the more fully they are discuss'd, the more firmly they will stand) yet I cannot but think it the Duty of the Civil Magistrate, at all Times, to take Care that Religion be not treated in a *ludicrous* or *reproachful* Manner, and effectually to discourage such Books and Writings as strike equally at the Foundation of all Religion, &c." What the *Bishop* of *L.* here says, of his *thinking it the Duty of the Civil Magistrate at all Times, to take Care that Religion be not treated in a ludicrous manner,* I understood as an Excuse for what he had done in stirring up the Civil Magistrate to a Prosecution of me; and that now, like a Philosopher, he was for letting Truth and Religion to take its Course, and for leaving it to a free Discussion, whether in a *ludicrous* or in a *calm, decent*

or *serious* Way. But I confess, I have mistaken the *Bishop*'s
Words, finding by Experience, that (for all the natural Import
of his Expression, that Liberty should be used to discuss the
Grounds of Religion in a *serious* Manner) he'll no more suffer it,
if he can help it, to be contested in a *serious,* than in a *ludicrous*
Way; wherefore else did he move for the Prosecution of a late
London Journal, which was all *calm, decent,* and *serious* Argument. And the Bishop of St. *David's* his furious *Dedication* now,
confirms me in this Opinion, that our *Clergy* (for all their
preaching up Liberty with as much Force and Strength of Reason as any Men, and for all their Invitations to *Infidels,* to say
and print their worst against Christianity) will by no means, if
they can hinder it, suffer any Attacks to be made upon their
Religion, nor cease their Importunities and Sollicitations of the
Civil Magistrate to Persecution. Blessed be God, the *Bishops* are
not my *Judges* as well as my *Accusers,* or I know, what would
become of me. . . .

I will here use no Arguments for Liberty of Debate, which
Subject has already been copiously handled, and wants nothing,
that I can add unto it. But before I enter into the Body of the
Bishop's Book, and upon a profess'd Defence of my Discourses
against him, let us consider the manifest Lies, Prevarications,
and wicked Insinuations in his *Dedication,* whereby he would
move the Secular Powers to a severe Punishment of me. I will
pass by the *Motto* of his Book, *viz. But Jesus said unto him,
Judas, betrayest thou the Son of Man with a Kiss;* Whereby he
would signify and intimate, not to *Scholars* (for they have more
Wit than to think the worse of me for his Abuse of Scripture)
but to the ignorant Multitude, that I am another *Judas,* a Trai-
tor and Rebel to *Jesus.* Commonly *Mottos* of Books are suited
to their Authors, and the Design of them; whether the *Bishop*
will be willing to take this *Motto* to himself or not, I will upon
another Occasion give it a pleasant and pertinent Turn upon
him. At present I shall only say, what the Learned will observe,
that *this* is of a wicked and malicious Use and Intention, of no
less, than to create in the Minds of the People an Hatred and
Detestation of me; of no other, than by dressing me up, as it
were, in a Bear's Skin, to excite the Ecclesiastical and merciless
Mob to worry and destroy me. Such has been the roguish Artifice

of Priests of all Ages, to represent their Adversaries, whom they would destroy, under odious and borrow'd Names, that their Persecutions of them might be thought the less cruel. But passing this by for the present, the

I. First wicked and wilful Misrepresentation that the *Bishop,* in his Dedication, has made of me, is that of being an *Infidel,* and an *Apostate* Clergyman. Wherefore else does he say thus to the Queen: "What is now presented to your Royal View, is an Apologetical Defence of our holy Religion, against one of the most virulent Libels on it, by an *Apostate Clergyman,* that has appear'd in any Christian Country; and in Comparison of which, other *Infidels* have acted a modest Part." And again he calls my *Discourses,* "A flagrant Sort of Profaneness, that tramples with Indignity on the Grounds of the Christian Faith." And again he signifies, "That I am warmly engaged in subverting the Christian Religion, and active in propogating Infidelity." This is all wilful and downright Calumny, to incense the Queen and the Government against me. The *Bishop* knows in his Heart that I am no *Infidel,* but a Believer of Christianity, notwithstanding my *Discourses* on Miracles, that have occasion'd such a Clamour against me. In my *Discourses,* I have repeatedly and most solemnly declared, that my Designs are not to do Service to Infidelity, but to advance the Glory of God, the Truth of Christianity, and to demonstrate the *Messiahship* of the holy *Jesus.* If I have sometimes ridiculed the litteral Story of our Saviour's Miracles, I have profess'd as often that it was with Design to turn Men's Hearts to the mystical Interpretation of them, on which alone *Jesus*'s Authority and Messiahship is founded. I could collect a great Number of Passages out of my *Discourses* to this Purpose, if it would not be wasting of Time and Paper. And do all these solemn Declarations of my Faith, and of the Integrity of my Heart, and of the Sincerity of my Intentions, stand for nothing? Why should not my Word here be taken? I can think of no other Reason, than because some other Folks are accustom'd to dissemble and prevaricate with God and Man in their Oaths and Subscriptions, therefore I may be suspected here of Hypocrisy, notwithstanding my Professions to the contrary.

Besides, the *Bishop* knows by my other Writings, that I am certainly a Christian, and a true Believer of the Religion of

Christ, though I may have some different Conceptions from other Men about it. It has been my good Luck before, not only to publish more Treatises purposely and professedly in Defence of Christianity, than any *Bishop* in *England;* but some of them are of such a Nature, as it's impossible for a Man to write without being a Christian, and impossible for him to depart from the Principles of them. This is my good Fortune and Happiness at this Juncture. The *Bishop* has perused, I see, some of my other Writings, and particularly, my *Old Apology for the Truth of Christianity revived;* and to his Praise, as well as my Comfort be it spoken, he apprehends and rightly relishes it. And as I was well pleased with his Representation of the Design of that Book, from the Principles and allegorical Scheme of which, he says (in Twenty-four Years since) I am not departed; so I would appeal to his Conscience, Whether a Man, who wrote, as I did then, of the Typical and Antitupal Deliverance of the *Jewish* and *Christian* Church, can possibly be an Infidel, or ever depart from the Christian Faith? If the *Bishop* has Ingenuity equal to his Penetration into that Book, he must own and confess to the World, that I was then, and am still a Christian, a Man of fix'd and unalterable Principles from that Day to this.

The *Bishop* would be thought in his *Preface* to enumerate all my Writings; but there are three others, whether wilfully or negligently omitted by him, I know not, that are direct Defences of the Truth of Christianity; and there is not a learned *Clergyman* in *England* (I humbly presume to say it) who can read them, and not applaud them. If the *Bishop* will be pleas'd to read one of them, *viz. The Defence of the Miracle of the Thundering Legion,* and say it from his Heart, that I might write that Book, and believe the Ecclesiatical Story of that Miracle, and yet be no Christian, then I will yield to his Accusation against me for Infidelity.

But why do I trouble my self thus to assert and vindicate my Belief of Christianity? The *Bishop* would readily come into the Acknowledgment of my being a sincere Christian, but for his Interests and Prejudices, and other political Considerations, which influence him and the *Clergy* so to decry and defame me, that, if possible, I must be destroy'd, or at least have my Mouth stopp'd.

In short then, it is not because I am an *Infidel,* that the *Clergy* so exclaim against me and my *Discourses;* but because, as a Christian, I have particular Designs in view, which, if I can compass, will tend to their Dishonour, and the Ruin of their Interests; and therefore, by Defamations and Prosecutions, they will, if they can, in time put a stop to them. The Designs that, for the Truth of Religion, and Good of Mankind, I have in view, and which, maugre all Opposition, Terrors, and Sufferings, I will pursue to the utmost of my Power, are these three.

1. To restore the Allegorical Interpretation of the Old and New Testament, that is call'd, say the Fathers, the sublime Mountain of Vision, on which we shall contemplate the Wisdom and Beauty of the Providence of God; and behold the glorious Transfiguration of *Jesus* with *Moses* and *Elias,* that is, the Harmony between the Gospel and the Law and the Prophets, agreeably to *Jesus*'s typical Transfiguration. And this is such a glorious and beatifick Vision, that it's enough to ravish our Hearts with the Hopes and Desires of attaining to it. The old *Jews* say, that the allegorical Interpretation of the Scriptures will lead us to the sight of God, and convert even *Atheists.* The Fathers say, that the allegorical Interpretation will be the Conversion of the *Jews* in the Perfection of Time; and St. *Augustin* speaks of a great allegorical *Genius,* that will be sent to that Purpose. I believe all this, and being convinced of the Truth of it, I am much addicted to Allegories. And it is plain enough, and wants no Proof, that the Revival of the allegorical Scheme, which I am fond of, portends Ruin to the *Ministry of the Letter;* and will be such an Argument of the Ignorance and Apostacy of our *Clergy,* that it's no wonder they defame, calumniate, and persecute me for my Attempts towards it.

Origen says, that *litteral Interpreters will run into Infidelity,* which is a Saying I am well pleased with, and thereupon will try if I can't turn the Tables upon our *Clergy;* I'll try if I can't shift from my self the present Load of Reproaches for Infidelity, and lay it upon them. . . .

I have indeed ludicrously treated the Letter of the Scriptures (in my *Discourses*) which by the said *Bishops* is falsely called *Blasphemy:* But should they either *ludicrously* or *sedately* write against the allegorical Sense of them, I could prove *that* to be real *Blasphemy*. However, I would not complain to the Civil Powers against them; no, it's God's peculiar Prerogative to punish that Sin, which ought not to be committed to the Care of the Civil Magistrate.

But what need I *ludicrously* to handle the Letter of our Saviour's Miracles? Because some Sort of Stories are the proper Subjects of *Ridicule;* and because . . . Ridicule will cut the Pate of an Ecclesiastical Numbskull, which calm and sedate Reasoning will make no Impression on.

To speak then the Truth in few Words. As I am resolv'd at any Rate to run down the *Letter,* in order to make way for the *Spirit* of the Scriptures, so certainly will our Clergy, for their Interests and Honour, as Ministers of the Letter, vilify and reproach me, and pursue me with an implacable Hatred: But I should think it meet for them to use a little more Temper in their Revilings, for fear the Torrent of Reproaches should sometime or other turn on them. It is asserted and predicted by the Fathers that, after a certain Time of the Church's Apostacy to the *Letter,* the *Spirit of Life,* or the allegorical Sense will re-enter the Scriptures, to the Advancement of divine Knowledge and true Religion; in the mean while the *Clergy* will do well to see to it. But,

2. The Second Design which, as a Christian, I have in View, and which occasionally I write for, is an universal and unbounded Toleration of Religion, without any Restrictions or Impositions on Men's Consciences; for which Design, the *Clergy* will hate and defame me, and, if possible, make an Infidel of me, as well as for the former. Upon an universal Toleration the World would be at quiet: That Hatred of one another, which is now so visible among different Sects, would then be terminated by a Unity of their Interests, when they are all upon the Level in the Eye of the Civil Magistrate, who would choose Men to Places of Trust, not for their Faith and Affection to Theological Doctrines, but for their Abilities to serve the Publick. In this Case, Ten thousand different *Notions* in Religion would no more obstruct the Welfare of the Community, than so many different *Noses* do the Happiness of this City. The Variety of their Theological Opinions, would be the Diversion and Amusement of each other; and so long as it was out of their Power to oppress,

they could not hate one another for them. Such a Toleration, the *Clergy* would persuade us, tends to Confusion and Distraction, as if Men would go to *Loggerheads* upon it. But this is one of their Mistakes; there would be a perfect Calm upon it, if such Incendiaries as they are did not disturb the publick Tranquillity. They'll tell us again, that such a Toleration makes Way for Dissoluteness of Morals, and would let in Sin like a Deluge upon us; but this is another of their Errors. Such a Toleration would promote Virtue; in as much as different Sects of Religion are a Check upon each other against Looseness of Morals, because every Sect would endeavour to approve itself above others, by the Goodness of their Lives, as well as by the Excellency of their Doctrine. But the *Clergy* will never hearken to such a Toleration, because it would be the Downfall of Ecclesiastical Power; for which Reason, among many others, I am

3. For the Abolition of an hired and establish'd Priesthood. And for this, if for nothing else, I am sure to be prosecuted with Hatred and Violence, and loaded with the Calumnies and Reproaches of Infidelity and Blasphemy: And the *Clergy,* if possible, will have my Mouth stopp'd, and my Hands tied, before I proceed too far in my Labours and Endeavours to this End.

And why should not the *Clergy* of the Church of *England* be turn'd to Grass, and be made to seek their Fortune among the People, as well as Preachers of other Denominations? Where's the Sense and Reason of imposing Parochial *Priests* upon the People to take care of their Souls, more than Parochial *Lawyers* to look to their Estates, or Parochial *Physicians* to attend their Bodies, or Parochial *Tinkers* to mend their Kettles? In secular Affairs every Man chooses the Artist and Mechanick that he likes best; so much more ought he in Spirituals, in as much as the Welfare of the Soul is of greater Importance than that of the Body or Estate. The Church-Lands would go a good, if not a full Step, towards the Payment of the Nation's Debts. . . .

In my first Discourse on Miracles, I happen'd to treat on that of Jesus's driving the Buyers and Sellers out of the Temple; which, upon the Authority of the Fathers, I shew'd to be a Figure of his future Ejection of Bishops, Priests, and

Deacons out of his Church, for making Merchandise of the
Gospel. The *Bishop* has taken me and that Miracle to task; and
if ever any Man smiled at another's Impertinence, I then heartily
laugh'd when I read him. I begg'd of the *Bishop* before-hand
not to meddle with that Miracle, because it was a hot one,
and would burn his Fingers. But for all my Caution, he has been
so Fool-hardy, as to venture upon it; but has really touch'd and
handled it, as if it was a *burning Coal*. He takes it up, and as
soon drops it again to blow his Fingers; then endeavours to
throw a little Water on *this* and *that* Part of it to cool it, but
all would not do. The most fiery Part of it, *viz.* that of its being
a Type of Jesus's future Ejection of mercenary Preachers out of
the Church, he has not, I may say it, at all touch'd, except by
calling it *my allegorical Invective against the Maintenance of the
Clergy;* which is such a Piece of *Corinthian* Effrontery in the
Bishop, that was he not resolv'd to lye and defame at all Rates,
for the Support of their Interests, he could never have had the
Face to have utter'd. If the *Bishop* had proved that *that* Miracle
(which litterally was such a————, as I dare not now call it)
neither was nor could be a Shadow and Resemblance of Jesus's
Ejection of hired Priests out of the Church at his second Advent,
and that the Fathers were not of this Opinion, he had knock'd
me down at once. As he has done nothing of this, so he might
have spared his Pains in Support of the Letter of this Story.
But I shall have a great deal of Diversion with the *Bishop,* when
I come, in a proper Place, to defend my Exposition of that
Miracle. In the mean Time, as the Bishop has publish'd one of
the Articles of my Christian Faith, thinking to render me odious
for it; so here I will insert another, *viz.* "I believe upon the
Authority of the Fathers, that the Spirit and Power of Jesus will
soon enter the Church, and expel Hireling Priests, who make
Merchandise of the Gospel, out of her, after the manner he is
supposed to have driven the *Buyers* and *Sellers* out of the
Temple."

Now upon all this, whether the *Bishop,* modestly speaking,
has not been unjust, uncharitable, and insincere, to represent
me as an *Infidel,* I appeal to all learned and ingenuous Gentle-
men. I am a Christian, though not upon the *litteral* Scheme,
which I nauseate, yet upon the *allegorical* one. And by the fol-

lowing easy and short Argument it may be proved that I am most certainly a Christian. I heartily and zealously contend for the allegorical Interpretation of the Scriptures, which the *Bishop* allows to be true of me; consequently I must, and do believe the Scriptures to be of divine Inspiration, or I could not think there were such Mysteries and Prophecy latent under the Letter of them. Whether then a Believer of the divine Inspiration of the Scriptures can be an Infidel (O most monstrous Paradox!) or any other than a Christian, judge Readers. Nay, if *Origen*'s and St. *Augustin*'s Testimony on my Behalf may be admitted, I am more truly a Christian and Disciple of the Holy Jesus, than any *litteral Schemist* can be. *Origen* says, That the Perfection of Christianity consists in a mystical Interpretation of the Old and New Testament, of the Historical, as well as other Parts of it. And St. *Augustin* says, That they who attain to the Understanding of the spiritual Signification of Jesus's Miracles, are the best Doctors in his School. The *Bishop* understands this Argument as well as any Man, and therefore I charge it home upon him, as a wilful and malicious Slander, to call and account me an Infidel in his *Dedication,* on purpose to incense the Government against me at this Juncture.

But the *Bishop* moreover calls me, as above, an *Apostate Clergyman;* And why so? Because I have deserted the *Ministry of the Letter,* and betaken my self to the *Ministry of the Spirit* of the Scriptures. That's like the Wit and Reasoning of his Pate! The *Bishop* is old enough, and has read enough to know that *Apostacy,* in the Sense of the Fathers, is a Desertion of the *Ministry of the Spirit,* and a Falling into the *Ministry of the Letter* of the Scriptures; whereupon I make bold to retort upon the *Bishop,* and say of him, and his Episcopal Brethren, that they are *Apostate Bishops. . . .*

*   *   *

. . . I must observe here, that besides my two *Bishops,* of *London* and St. *David's,* (and some other inconsiderable *Triflers*) there are two *anonymous* Authors against me, whose Works have acquir'd some Fame. The One is intitled, *The Miracles of Jesus vindicated,* in *Three Parts.* If I could have gotten to the certain Knowledge of the Author, I should have

been tempted to have had a Bout with him; and to have ex-
postulated with him, both with Regard to his Arguments and
good Manners. I would have taught him a better Use, and a
more proper Application of the Words *Dishonesty, and want of
Honesty,* than to reproach me with them. Common Fame says,
Dr. *Pearse,* of St. *Martin's,* is the Author; but I am apt to think,
the *King's* Parish Priest, and other City *Divines,* have more Wit
and Craft than to upbraid me as above, for fear a just Charge
of *Dishonesty,* for their Extortions and Exactions on the People,
should be retorted on them. Upon the Publication of the *First
Part* of the foresaid Treatise, my *Jewish Rabbi* comes to me in
all haste, saying to me, "Look you here, do you see how this
Author has new vampt the old *mumpsimus* Argument of *Jesus's*
Resurrection? Do you observe how imperfectly, here and there,
he answers my Objections to it; and silently slips by some knotty
Pieces of them, that were too hard for him to untie?" Yes,
Rabbi, said I, I do observe all this; (and what I have observ'd
since, he argues, awkwardly and backwardly, for the Certainty
of *Jesus's* other Miracles, from his Resurrection). My *Rabbi*
presently re-inforc'd his Resurrection-Objection against this Author, and would have had me to print it. No, no, *Rabbi,* said I;
you may print it your self, if you dare. I must wait to hear how
Causes will go in *Westminster-Hall,* next Term, before I involve
my self in another Law-Suit. Besides, *Rabbi,* they say, I don't
really thus correspond with a *Jew,* but do only personate one;
and the *Bishop* of St. *David's* hints, that I am answerable to
publick Justice for so doing. Here my Rabbi stampt with
Indignation; saying, What if you did personate a *Jew?* Is it not
lawful, and in Use with your *Divines,* to write Conferences between a Christian and a *Jew?* And do you any more in this
Case? Yes, *Rabbi,* said I, it is lawful to write such-like Conferences, and to make *Jewish* Objections to Christianity, when
they are no stronger than may be easily dissipated: But when
Men write from the Heart, as you do, and raise a D---l that our
Clergy can't easily lay, it is, they say, intolerable, and punish-
able; and either you or I, in the Opinion of the *Bishop,* ought
to suffer for it.

The other considerable *Treatise* against me, is that of *The
Trial of the Witnesses of the Resurrection of Jesus;* which is an

ingenious Piece, and I was well pleased with it. Some time after the Publication of this *Treatise*, I made my Jewish *Rabbi* a Visit, when, drinking a *Dish* of *Tea* together, we talk'd it over; and my *Rabbi* was pleas'd to deliver his Sentiments of it in this fashion: "Whoever was the Author of this Treatise, God knows, but he's certainly a Friend to my Objections against *Jesus*'s Resurrection, which he has fairly stated; but is so far from fully confuting all of them, that he discovers a Consciousness, here and there, that they are unanswerable. It is commonly reported that Bishop *Sherlock* is the Author of this *Treatise*, but this Report I look upon as an Artifice of the Booksellers, to make it sell well; or rather the Author's contrived *Banter* upon the *Clergy*, and their weak Christian Brethren, to try how far they may be imposed on, and drawn into the Approbation and Admiration of a Treatise, that really makes against them. There is but very little in this Treatise, to make it reputed a sufficient Answer to my Objections, excepting the Verdict of the *Jury*, who brought in the Witnesses of the Resurrection, *Not Guilty*, of either Fraud or Mistake in it. *Bishop Sherlock* can't be the Author of this Treatise, if for no other Reason than this, that *that* Author is visibly against that Ecclesiastical Wealth and Power, which the *Bishop* is possess'd of, and does think not disagreeable to the Mind of Christ and his poor Apostles. In any *Bishop* is the concealed Author of this Treatise, he must secretly be of the Opinion of the atheistical Pope, who said, *quantum nobis prosuit hæc de Christo Fabula*, what vast Advantage has the Story of Christ been to us Popes and Bishops." I readily gave into the Opinion of my *Rabbi*, and wonder'd, *Bishop Sherlock* did not so much as by a publick Advertisement clear himself of being the Author of this Treatise, and so put a Stop to the Report. It may be the *Bishop* is above the Scandal of it; but I was so concern'd for his Reputation, that I drew up a *Vindication* of him from the Slander of it; which I had publish'd, but for my *Rabbi*'s farther Thoughts about the Resurrection of Jesus inserted in it, that our *Bishops* might have possibly taken Offence at. So I dropp'd that Design at present, but hope still for an Opportunity to publish the said Vindication of the *Bishop*, by which, I don't doubt, but to merit his Friendship and Favour.

But whoever was the real Author of the foresaid Treatise, I

humbly and heartily beg of him to publish, what in the Conclusion of it, he has given us some Hopes of, *The Trial of the Witnesses of the Resurrection of* LAZARUS, because my *Rabbi*'s Objections to it are a Novelty and Curiosity, which, by way of such a Reply to them, I should be glad to see handled. . . .

If it please God, that I enjoy Life, Health, and Liberty, I'll go on with my Designs. I am resolv'd to give the *Letter* of the Scriptures no Rest, so long as I am able by Reason and Authority to disturb it. If our Ministers of the *Letter* will not ascend with me, the sublime and allegorical *Mountain* of divine Contemplation, they shall have no Comfort nor Enjoyment of themselves in the low *Valley* of the *Letter,* if I can disquiet them. Notwithstanding what the *Bishop* has written in *Vindication* of *Jesus*'s Miracles, the litteral Story of them, by the Leave of God, and of the Civil Magistrate, shall be afresh attack'd, and perhaps with more *Ridicule,* than I used before. What should I flinch for? The litteral Story of *Jesus*'s Miracles is not, in the Opinion of the Fathers, as well as of my self, agreeable to Sense and Reason; neither can *Jesus*'s Authority and Messiahship be founded on the *Letter* of them. I am not for the *Messiahship* of a carnal *Jesus,* who cured the bodily Diseases of Blindness and Lameness; but for the Messiahship of the spiritual *Jesus,* who will cure the Blindness and Lameness of our Understandings. I am for the Messiahship of the spiritual *Jesus,* who will expel the mercenary Preachers out of his Church, after the manner that *Jesus* in the Flesh is supposed to have driven the Sellers out of the Temple, which litterally is but a sorry Story. I am for the Messiahship of the spiritual *Jesus,* who exorcised the furious and persecuting Devils out of the Mad-men of *Jews* and *Gentiles;* and tho' he permitted them to enter into a Herd of Ecclesiastical Swine, yet will precipitate them into the Sea of Divine Knowledge. I am for the spiritual *Jesus,* who will cure the *Woman* of the Church, of her *Issue of Blood,* that is shed in Persecution and War; which her Ecclesiastical Physicians, and Quack-Doctors of the *Clergy,* have not been able to do, tho' they have received large Fees and Revenues to that End. I am for a spiritual *Messiah,* who will cure the Woman of the Church of her *Infirmity,* at the Spirit of Prophecy, of whose Infirmity this Age is her *eighteenth* Year. So could I write of all *Jesus*'s Miracles; for the whole Evangelical History is Figure and Shadow of the spiritual *Jesus,* whom we should *know to be in us of a Truth, unless we be Reprobates.* The *Clergy,* if they are not wilfully blind, may hence see my Christian Faith and Principles; and be assured, that what I do in this Controversy, is with a View to the Honour of God, the Advancement of Truth, the Edification of the Church, and Demonstration of the Messiahship of the Holy *Jesus,* to whom be Glory for ever. *Amen.*

English Deism in Decline

After the writings of Woolston and Tindal, English deism went into slow decline. There are three reasons for this decline: by the 1730s, nearly all the arguments in behalf of deism, both critical and constructive, had been offered and refined; the intellectual caliber of leading deists was none too impressive; and the opponents of deism finally mustered some formidable spokesmen. The deists of these decades, Peter Annet (1693-1769), Thomas Chubb (1679-1747), and Thomas Morgan (?-1743), are of significance to the specialist alone. Simply, and often brutally, they restated the old deist critique of the miracles, while some of them, like Morgan, insisted that their deism was "Christian." It had all been said before, and better.

The only significant exception to the dreary parade was Conyers Middleton (1683-1750), an intelligent and respected scholar; but his allegiance to deism was problematic, for with his historical mentality he challenged not merely the supposedly eternal validity of miracles, but also the unhistorical mentality of the deists. Middleton acquired some notoriety with his *A Letter from Rome,* a virulent but circumstantial and powerful attack on "Popish superstition," which makes its point in the subtitle: *Shewing an Exact Conformity between Popery and Paganism, or, The Religion of the Present Romans, derived from that of their Heathen Ancestors* (1729). It went through several editions—the fourth, published in 1741, while he was chief librarian of Cambridge University, attests to the enduring popularity of the pamphlet. But Middleton's chief work is the *Free Inquiry Into the Miraculous Powers, Which are supposed to have subsisted in the Christian Church, From the Earliest Ages through several successive Centuries, By which it is shewn, That we have no sufficient Reason to believe, upon the Authority of the Primitive Fathers, That any such Powers were continued to the Church after the Days of the Apostles* (1748). Here was historical criticism in germ: Middleton placed the early Fathers into their age, and their practices and beliefs into the religious context of a superstitious time.

This argument gave considerable support to the deists, but it also struck at the root of their position. The deists were unhistorical in their view of man and religion. Simple unspoiled man, they believed, can grasp religious truths by his own untutored intuition, for the truths that God wants man to know are basically simple. Hence the primitive Christians, expressing their beliefs before corrupt and cunning priests had filled Christianity with lies and absurd ceremonies, must be somehow superior to modern Christians in their insight into religious truth. Middleton, with his historical method, ruined this deist argument.

Actually, while he wrote, the deists had already suffered another serious attack, from the hands of an undoubted Christian and prominent churchman, Bishop Joseph Butler (1692-1752). Butler was a skilled philosopher and a generous antagonist—he even recommended the essays of that notorious infidel David Hume. In 1726, he published *Fifteen Sermons,* which established him as a moral philosopher; and in 1736, he published *The Analogy of Religion, Natural and Revealed, to the Constitution and Course of Nature,* his most famous work. It argued, in substance, that God has revealed himself in the course of natural events, and that the God of the deists (who speaks through his natural works) and the God of the Christians (who speaks through special providences and particular miracles) is the same. The strength of Butler's argument was the reliance on man's moral nature, from which he reasoned to the moral constitution of the universe, a constitution that could only have been granted by the very God Who is revealed in Scriptures. The appeal to experience, on which deists had long relied, is here taken away from them and employed in behalf of reasonable—Anglican—Christianity.

This was not the worst. The heaviest blows fell on the deists from a self-proclaimed infidel, David Hume. In the 1730s, while still a young man, Hume had elaborated a notorious argument against miracles, which he published in 1748, as part of his *Philosophical Essays Concerning Human Understanding.* The argument, which is hard to summarize and remains worth reading, held not that miracles were impossible. It did not even hold that miracles had never taken place. It merely asserted that no miracles so far reported deserved credence: the men who attested to them, coupled with man's natural penchant for believing the unusual, made every report suspect.

In addition to this argument, Hume sprinkled his writings with sardonic remarks about priestcraft, and in general was considered a complete infidel, a name in which he rather wryly rejoiced. But he was not a deist, for he was too skeptical to accept the deists' belief in the wisdom of primitive man, or their certainty about the fatherly government of a God. He attacked the first of these tenets in his brilliant essay, "The Natural History of Religion" (1757) in which he argues that primitive man must have been a polytheist, and that theism—the ancestor of deism— was the result of long cultivation; and he demolished the second in his equally brilliant *Dialogues Concerning Natural Religion,* written and rewritten in the 1750s, but suppressed at the wishes of his anxious friends, and not published until 1779, three years after Hume's death. It is a great work, which examines with devastating effect the favorite deist metaphor of God the Watchmaker. This analogy is weak, Hume suggests, as all analogies are; but if one *is* to seek for an analogy for the nature of God in the affairs of the world, one would not think Him a Watchmaker, but an organism, like a vegetable. Like the "Natural History of Religion," the *Dialogues* must be read and should not be summarized.

However effective the *Dialogues* seem to us, they had little effect, and aroused little stir in 1779 when they were published. The deist debate was over, in England at least. But on the Continent it was still in full swing.

C. DEISM ON THE CONTINENT

Sermon of the Fifty*

Voltaire

Continental deism is a curious mixture of import and native product. Sixteenth-century skeptics like Montaigne and the very different seventeenth-century skeptic Bayle allowed adventurous readers to experiment with their own versions of natural religion, reinforced by an anticlericalism that needed no books to stimulate it. In addition, in some severely restricted circles, society poets circulated unprintable poems ridiculing the Churches, and blaspheming the Virgin Mary and the Savior himself. When Voltaire went to England in 1726, he had already absorbed a good deal of this propaganda; he was ready for English deism.

But English deism, it seems, traveled well. French visitors would return with reports of impious conversation, or copies of impious pamphlets or poems (like Pope's somewhat ambiguous "Essay on Man"). Deists readily found translators: Collins' Discourse of Free-Thinking *was translated into French in 1714,* Tindal's Christianity as Old as the Creation, *into German in 1741. As deism waned in England, it waxed in France and the German states.*

Voltaire was not the first of the French deists—his great precursor Montesquieu professed a naturalistic religion much like deism—but he was the most celebrated; if deism kept its hold over the Continent for so long, this was at least in part the result of Voltaire's brilliance as a stylist and diligence as a writer.

Born in 1694 to a prominent middle-class family in Paris, Voltaire was educated by the Jesuits and early showed passion

---

* From *Sermon des cinquante,* in *Œuvres,* ed. Armand-Aubrée (1829), XXVI, 323-343 *passim.* Translated by Peter Gay (I have profitably consulted the fine translation and critical edition, *The Sermon of the Fifty,* ed. J. A. R. Séguin [1962]).

and talent for letters. He associated with elegant degenerate circles in Paris and the châteaux around the city and there strengthened his youthful impiety. In 1718, he brought out his first play, the tragedy Œdipe, which made him famous. It is not precisely a deist play, but the propaganda against intolerance and the rebellion against a cruel God are strong in it. Voltaire expressed this point of view—an informal deism, one might say— once more, poetically, in his long epic on king Henri IV, the Henriade, *completed in several versions in the 1720s: Henri IV is a great king because he sees the virtue of tolerance and the viciousness of the priesthood. The poem, like the play that preceded it, gave Voltaire the reputation of a classical author in modern dress.*

Then, in 1726, Voltaire went to England and stayed for more than two years. He did not become a deist there; he was a deist when he arrived. But he gathered knowledge and ammunition there. An important result was his celebrated book on England, the Lettres philosophiques *(first published in full in 1734), which is not yet open deist propaganda, but which speaks well of English tolerance and rather amusingly singles out the Quakers for praise, for their decency, their odd habits, their freedom from absurd religious superstitions. Voltaire did not yet dare go further than that; he had gone indeed far enough: the book was burned as impious and seditious.*

Through the 1730s and 1740s, Voltaire spent much of his time at the château of Cirey with his bluestocking mistress, the Madame du Châtelet, with whom he studied the Bible and commentaries on the Bible from many points of view. It was not until the 1750s, probably in 1750-2, when Voltaire was a guest of Frederick II of Prussia, that he finally wrote down in polemical form what he believed about God, eternal justic, tolerance, persecution, and fanaticism. It was probably at the court of Frederick the Great that he wrote his Sermon of the Fifty, *and the first articles of the* Philosophical Dictionary, *but it was not until the 1760s, when he was rather safely settled on his property at Ferney, just a short ride away from Genevan territory, that he began to publish what he had thought for forty, and written down for twenty years.*

The last decades of Voltaire's life are a deluge of deist propa-

ganda, connected closely with his humanitarian causes, and de-
mands for all kinds of reform—especially legal reform. He wrote
literally scores of deist pamphlets, using many different names
and many different devices. But the arguments are always the
same; critically: the Jewish religion is the despicable mother of
the despicable Christian religion; the Bible is a compilation of
incredible and unworthy tales; churches in all ages and countries
are filled with vicious and rapacious priests; miracles are fairy
tales invented by fools and embroidered by politicians. And con-
structively: there is a God who made the world with justice, en-
joins men to respect Him and respect Him by following his simple
and rational laws; the laws of God and nature can be discovered
with ease—here Voltaire respectfully disagrees with David Hume
—and followed by all men not corrupted by the priest-ridden
world in which they live. There is only one thing men must know:
be just.

For a year, fifty well educated, pious, and reasonable persons
have been gathering every Sunday in a populous and mercantile
town. They say prayers, and afterwards a member of the society
delivers a talk. Then they have dinner, and after the meal they
take up a collection for the poor. Each presides in his turn;
it is up to the president to say the prayer and give the sermon.
Here is one of these prayers and one of these sermons.

If the seeds of these words should drop into good soil, surely
they will bear fruit.

PRAYER

God of all worlds and all beings, the only prayer that can be
agreeable to you is submission; for what should one ask of the
one who has ordained everything, foreseen everything, connected
everything from the beginning of things? If, however, it is permitted to expose one's needs to a father, let us preserve in our
hearts this very submission, let us preserve your pure religion;
and keep us free from all superstition. If one can insult you by
unworthy sacrifices, then abolish those sordid mysteries; if one
can dishonor the Divinity with absurd fables, may these fables
perish forever; if the days of the prince and the magistrate are

not counted from all eternity, lengthen the duration of their days;
preserve the purity of our morals, the friendship our brethren
have for one another, the benevolence they feel to all men, their
obedience to the laws, and their wisdom in private conduct; may
they live and die worshipping one God alone, a God who rewards the good and avenges evil, a God who cannot have been
born or died, or have had associates, but who has too many
rebellious children in this world.

SERMON

My brethren, religion is the secret voice of God which speaks
to all men; it should unite, and not divide, them all; hence any
religion that belongs to only one people is false. Ours is in its
basic principle the religion of the entire universe; for we worship a Supreme Being as all nations worship him, we practice
the justice that all nations teach, and we reject all those lies
with which all nations reproach one another: thus, in agreement
with them in the principle that reconciles them, we differ from
them in the matters over which they fight.

It is impossible that the point on which all men in all ages
agree should not be the single center of the truth, and that the
points in which they all differ should not be the standards of
falsehood. Religion must be in conformity with morality, and,
like it, universal; hence every religion whose dogmas offend
against morality is surely false. It is under this double aspect
of perversity and falsity that we shall examine in this discourse
the books of the Hebrews and of those who succeeded them.
Let us see first of all if these books do conform with morality;
after that we shall see if they can have a shadow of plausibility.
The two first points will deal with the Old Testament, and the
third with the New.

FIRST POINT

My brethren, you know what horror seized us when we read
the writings of the Hebrews together, directing our attention
only to those traits that violated purity, charity, good faith, justice, and universal reason, traits we found not merely in every
chapter but which, to make things worse, were sanctified in all.

First, not saying a word about the extravagant injustice which they dare to impute to the Supreme Being—having endowed a snake with speech to seduce a woman and ruining the innocent descendants of that woman!—let us follow, step by step, all the historical horrors, which are repellent to nature and good sense. One of the first patriarchs, Lot, Abraham's nephew, receives in his house two angels disguised as pilgrims; the inhabitants of Sodom develop a lewd desire for the two angels; Lot, who had two daughters promised in marriage, offers to prostitute them to the people in place of these two strangers. These girls must have been singularly used to being prostitutes, since the first thing they do after their city is consumed by a rain of fire and their mother has been transformed into a statue of salt, is to get their father drunk for two nights in a row to sleep with him one after the other. This is an imitation of the ancient Arabic fable of Cyniras and Myrrha; but in that far more decent fable, Myrrha is punished for her crime while Lot's daughters are rewarded with the greatest and dearest blessing (according to the Jewish mind): they become mothers of numerous descendants.

We will not linger over the lie of Isaac—Isaac, father of the just—who says that his wife is his sister; perhaps he merely revived Abraham's lie, perhaps Abraham was actually guilty of making his sister into his wife. But let us dwell for a moment on the patriarch Jacob, who is held up to us as the model of men. He forces his brother, who is starving, to give up to him his birthright for a dish of lentils; after that he deceives his aged father on his deathbed; and after he has deceived his father, he deceives and robs his father-in-law, Laban: to marry two sisters is nothing—he sleeps with all his servants, and God blesses this incontinence and these impostures. What are the actions of the children of such a father? Dinah, his daughter, pleases a prince of Shechem, and it is probable that she loves this prince, for she sleeps with him. The prince asks her in marriage, and his request is granted on condition that he and his nation have themselves circumcised. The prince accepts this proposition; but as soon as he and his men have undergone this painful operation—which still must have left them with enough strength to defend themselves—Jacob's family cuts the throats of all the men of Shechem, and turns the women and children into slaves.

In our childhood we all heard the story of Thyestes and Pelops; that incestuous abomination is revived in Judah, the patriarch and father of the first tribe: he sleeps with his daughter-in-law and after that wants to have her killed. After this, the book relates that Joseph, a child in this wandering family, is sold into Egypt, and that this stranger is established there as prime minister for having explained a dream. But what kind of prime minister is this man who, in a time of famine, compels a whole nation to enslave itself that it may have bread! What magistrate in our country would dare to suggest such an abominable bargain in time of famine? And what nation would accept such a sordid bargain? Let us here not look into just how seventy persons of the family of Joseph who had settled in Egypt, could have multiplied to six hundred thousand able-bodied soldiers (not counting women, children, and the aged) in the course of two hundred and fifteen years—that adds up to a multitude of nearly two million souls. Let us not discuss how the text gives four hundred and thirty years, when the same text used to give two hundred and fifteen. The infinite number of contradictions which are the mark of imposture is not the subject that should detain us here. Let us also forget about the ridiculous prodigies performed by Moses and the Pharaoh's wizards, and all those miracles performed to give the Jewish people, instead of the fertile land of Egypt where they were, a miserable spot of poor soil, which they later acquired with blood and crime. Let us concentrate on that frightful path of iniquity which they were made to tread. Their God made Jacob a thief, and he made a whole people into thieves; he ordered his people to steal and carry off all the vessels of gold and silver, and all the utensils of the Egyptians. Look at these poor wretches, numbering six hundred thousand able bodied soldiers who, instead of taking up arms like men of courage, flee like brigands, led by their God. If that God had wanted to give them a good land, he could have given them Egypt; but no: he leads them into a desert. They could have saved themselves by the shortest route, but they make a detour of more than thirty miles to cross the Red Sea with dry feet. After that fine miracle, Moses's own brother makes them another god, and that god is a calf. To punish his brother, the same Moses orders priests to kill their sons, their brothers, and their fathers, and these priests kill twenty-three thousand Jews, who let themselves be slaughtered like cattle.

After this butchery, it is not surprising that this abominable people should sacrifice human victims to its God, whom they call *Adonaï,* from the name *Adonis,* which they borrowed from the Phoenicians. Verse 29 of chapter XXVII in Leviticus expressly prohibits the redemption of men consecrated to the anathema of sacrifice, and it is in accord with this cannibalist law that Jephthah will some time later immolate his own daughter.

To cut the throats of twenty-three thousand men for a calf is not enough; besides, we can count twenty-four thousand others, immolated for having had intercourse with idolatrous girls: a worthy prelude, a worthy example, my brethren, of religious persecutions.

This people advances through the deserts and rocks of Palestine. "Here is your lovely country," God tells them: "murder all the inhabitants, kill all the male children, put the married women to death, keep all the little girls in reserve for yourselves." All this is carried out to the letter, according to the Hebrew books; and we would shudder with horror at this recital, if the text did not add that the Jews found 675,000 sheep, 72,000 oxen, 61,000 asses, and 32,000 virgins in the Midianite camp. Happily, absurdity here gives the lie to barbarism; but, once again, it is not here that I wish to examine the ridiculous and the impossible; I concentrate on the execrable.

Let us not emphasize, my dear brothers, the innumerable barbarities of the kings of Judah and Israel, the murders, the assaults always coupled with ridiculous stories—ridiculous, but always bloody. Even the prophet Elisha found it necessary to be barbarous. This worthy pious man had forty children devoured by bears, because these little innocents had called him "baldy." Let us leave this abominable nation in its Babylonian captivity, and in its slavery under the Romans, with all the fine promises of their god Adonis or Adonaï, who had so often assured the Jews that they would rule the whole world. Finally, under the wise government of the Romans, a king was born to the Hebrews, and that king, my brethren, that *shilo,* that Messiah— you know who he is: he is a man who had first been numbered among the large number of prophets without a mission who, not being priests, made a living being inspired; at the end of several centuries, he was finally regarded as a God. Let us go no farther; let us see on what pretexts, on what facts, on what miracles, on what predictions, in a word on what foundation this disgusting and abominable story is constructed.

SECOND POINT

O my God! if you were to descend to earth, if you were to order me to believe this tissue of murders, thefts, assaults, incests, committed on your order and in your name, I would say: "No, your sanctity does not ask me to acquiesce in these horrible things which insult you; surely you wish to test me."

How then, virtuous and wise listeners, can we believe that dreadful history with the pitiful evidence that remains behind?

Let us quickly peruse the books so falsely attributed to Moses: I say, falsely, for it is not possible that Moses should have spoken of things that happened long after him; none of us would believe that the memoirs of William, Prince of Orange, were by his hand if these memoirs spoke of events that occurred after his death. Let us peruse, I say, what we have been told under the name of Moses. In the beginning, God made the light which he called *day,* then the shadows which he called *night,* and that was the first day. Hence there were days before the sun had been created.

Then, on the sixth day, God made man and woman; but as the Author forgot that the woman had already been made, he then drags her from one of Adam's ribs. Adam and Eve are put in a garden from which rise four rivers; and among these four rivers there are two, the Euphrates and the Nile, which have their source more than two thousand miles from each other. The serpent then spoke like a man; it was the cleverest of the animals of the fields; it persuades the woman to eat an apple, and in this way has her chased from paradise. Mankind multiplied, and the children of God fell in love with the daughters of men. There were giants on the earth, and God regretted that he had made man; he therefore wanted to exterminate him by the flood. But he wanted to save Noah, and ordered him to make a vessel of poplar, three hundred cubits long: seven pairs of all the clean animals, and two of the unclean ones, had to enter into this single vessel. They had therefore to be fed for ten months while the water covered the earth. Now, you can see what would have been needed to feed fourteen elephants, four-teen camels, fourteen buffaloes, as many horses, asses, elks, stags, deer, serpents, ostriches—in a word, more than two thousand species. You ask me where the water came from to cover the whole earth, fifteen cubits above the highest mountains. The text replies that it was taken from the cataracts of the heavens. God knows where those cataracts are. After the deluge, God made an alliance with Noah, and with all the animals; and, to confirm this alliance, he established the rainbow.

Those who wrote this were not great physicists—as you can see. Here then is Noah, with a religion given him by God, and that religion is neither the Jewish nor the Christian religion. Noah's descendants tried to build a tower that would reach up to heaven: a fine enterprise! God is afraid of it; in a moment he has the workmen speaking several different languages, and they disperse. All this is in this antique oriental taste. . . .

This, then, is the Old Testament, from one end to the other; it is the father of the New, a father who disavows his son and considers him a bastard and a rebellious child; for the Jews, faithful to the law of Moses, look with execration upon Christi-anity, built on the ruins of that law. But the Christians have, with quibbles, tried to justify the New Testament by this very Old Testament. Thus, these two religions fight each other with the same weapons; they call to witness the same prophets; they claim the same predictions.

Will future centuries, which will have seen the end of such mad cults and which perhaps—alas!—will have seen others no less unworthy of God and men, be able to believe that Judaism and Christianity rested on such foundations, on such prophecies? And what prophecies! Listen: the prophet Isaiah is called by King Ahaz, king of Judah, to offer some predictions, in the vain and superstitious manner of the whole Orient—for these prophets, as you know, were persons who got mixed up in the business of divination in order to make a living, just as there were still many of them in Europe in the last century, above all among the lower orders. Besieged in Jerusalem by Shalmaneser who had taken Samaria, King Ahaz asked the seer for a prophecy and a sign. Isaiah told him: "Behold the sign: A girl shall conceive; she will have a son whose name will be Emmanuel; he will eat butter and honey until the time he will know how to reject evil and choose good; and before that child will have reached that stage, the land you hold in detestation will be abandoned by its two kings, and the Eternal will whistle for the flies that live on the banks of the rivers of Egypt and Assyria; he will shave the beard of the Assyrian king with a rented razor; he will shave his head and the hair on his feet."

After this fine prediction reported in Isaiah (of which there is not a word in the Book of Kings), the prophet himself is ordered to carry it out. The Lord first of all orders him to write on a great scroll that one ought to plunder quickly: he plunders quickly and then, in the presence of witnesses, he sleeps with a girl and gets her with child; but instead of calling it Emmanuel, he calls it Maher-shalal-hash-baz. This then, my brethren, is what the Christians have twisted in favor of their Christ: this then is the prophecy on which Christianity is founded. The girl whom the prophet got with child is unquestionably the Virgin Mary; Maher-shalal-hash-baz is Jesus Christ. As for the butter and honey: I have no idea what that is supposed to be. Every seer predicted to the Jews that they should be delivered from their captivity, and, according to the Christians, this deliverance is the celestial Jerusalem and the Church of our day. With the Jews everything is prophecy; but with the Christians everything is a miracle, and all these prophecies are prefigurations of Jesus Christ.

Here, my brethren, is one of those lovely and striking prophecies: the great prophet Ezekiel saw the northern gale, and four animals, and wheels of chrysolite all full of eyes, and the Eternal said to him: "Arise, eat a book, and then go off."

The Eternal orders him to sleep for three hundred and ninety days on his left side, and then forty on the right side. The Eternal ties him up with ropes; certainly this prophet was a man who should have been tied up—but we are not yet finished. Can I repeat without vomiting what God commands Ezekiel to do? I must do it. God commands him to eat barley bread cooked with shit. Is it credible that the filthiest scoundrel of our time could imagine such excremental rubbish? Yes, my brethren, the prophet eats his barley bread with his own excrement: he complains that this breakfast disgusts him a little and God, as a conciliatory gesture, permits him to mix his bread with cow dung instead. Here then is a prototype, a prefiguration of the Church of Jesus Christ.

After this instance it is not necessary to offer others, and to waste our time battling against all the disgusting and abominable fantasies controverted among Jews and Christians: let us content ourselves with deploring the most lamentable blindness that has ever afflicted human reason; let us hope that this blindness will pass like so many others; and let us turn to the New Testament, worthy sequel to what we have just discussed.

THIRD POINT

It was in vain that the Jews should have been a little more enlightened in the time of Augustus than in those barbarous centuries of which we have just spoken: it was in vain that the Jews should have begun to believe in the immortality of the soul (a doctrine unknown to Moses), and in divine rewards after death for the just as well as punishments, whatever they might be, for the wicked (a doctrine no less unknown to Moses). Reason, for all this, did not penetrate among the miserable nation from which emerged that Christian religion, which has been the source of so many quarrels, of civil wars and crimes, which has spilled so much blood, and which is divided into so many hostile sects in the corners of the world where it reigns.

Among the Jews there have always been men from the rabble who played at being prophets in order to distinguish themselves from the mob: here then is the one who made the most noise, and who was turned into a god. Here in a few words is the summary of his career, as it is reported in the books they call the Gospels. Let us not seek to know at what time these books were written, although it is obvious that they were written after the fall of Jerusalem. You know how absurdly the four authors contradict one another; this is conclusive proof of falsehood. Alas! we have no need of so many proofs to ruin this miserable edifice; let us content ourselves with a short and faithful report.

First of all Jesus is made into a descendant of Abraham and

David, and the author Matthew counts forty-two generations in
two thousand years; but in his account we find only forty-one,
and in this genealogical tree, which he takes from the Book of
Kings, he still makes a grave mistake by calling Josiah the father
of Jeconiah.

Luke also offers a genealogy; but he gives fifty-six generations
from Abraham, and these are entirely different generations.
Finally, to top it all off, these genealogies are connected to Joseph,
but the evangelists claim that Jesus was not of Joseph's descendants! In truth, would one be admitted to a Chapter of the German
Empire on such proofs of nobility? And this involves the Son of
God! and God himself is the author of this book!

Matthew says that when Jesus, king of the Jews, was born in
a stable in the town of Bethlehem, three magi or three kings
saw his star in the Orient, that they followed that star which
stopped at Bethlehem, and that King Herod, having heard about
these things, had all the children under two massacred. Could
there be a more ridiculous horror? Matthew adds that the father
and mother took their little boy into Egypt and remained there
until the death of Herod. Luke explicitly says the opposite: he
notes that Joseph and Mary remained peaceably in Bethlehem
for six weeks, then went to Jerusalem, from there to Nazareth,
and that every year they went to Jerusalem.

The evangelists contradict one another about the length of
Jesus's life, about the miracles, about the day of the last supper,
about that of his death, about the apparitions after his death—
in a word, about almost all the facts. The Christians of the early
centuries made forty-nine gospels which all contradict one another
even more: in the end, they picked the four gospels which remain to us; but even if they all agreed, great God! what absurdities! what trifles! what puerile and hateful things!

Jesus's first adventure, that is to say, God's son's first adventure,
is to be kidnapped by the devil; for the devil, who had not appeared in the books of Moses, plays a major role in the Gospels.
The devil, then, carries off God to a mountain in the desert; he
shows him, from there, all the kingdoms of the earth. Which is
the mountain from which one can see so many countries? We
haven't the slightest idea.

John reports that Jesus goes to a wedding and changes water

into wine; that he chases from the temple court all those who sell animals for the sacrifices commanded by the Law.

All illnesses in those days were possessions of the devil; and in fact Jesus assigns to his apostles the task of chasing out devils. Thus he casually delivers a man possessed by a legion of demons, and he makes these demons enter a herd of swine, which throw themselves into the Lake of Tiberias: we may guess that the owners of these swine, who apparently were not Jews, were not amused by this trick. He heals a blind man, and that blind man sees human beings as though they were trees. He wants to eat figs in the winter, he looks for some on a fig-tree, and as he finds none, he curses the tree and has it dry up. The text does not fail to add prudently: "For it was not the time for figs."

He transforms himself at night, he makes Moses and Elijah appear. . . . In truth, do sorcerers' tales even approach such absurdities? This man who continually insulted the Pharisees, who called them "generations of vipers," "whitened sepulchres," is finally turned over to the courts by them, and put to death with two thieves; and his historians have the nerve to tell us that at his death the earth was covered with darkness at noon, when there was a full moon; as if all the writers of that time would not have mentioned such a strange miracle.

After all this, it is a mere nothing to have him call himself resurrected, and to predict the end of the world, which however has not yet come.

The sect of this Jesus subsisted in hiding, but fanaticism made it grow; at the beginning they do not dare to make this man a God, but soon their boldness increases. Some parts of Plato's metaphysics are mixed in with the Nazarene sect; Jesus is turned into the *logos,* the Word-God, consubstantial with God his father. They imagine the Trinity, and to make it credible, they falsify the earliest gospels.

They add a passage about this Trinity; just as they falsify the historian Josephus, to have him say a word about Jesus, even though Josephus is too serious a historian to have mentioned such a man. They go so far as to make up Sybilline verses: they make up Apostolic canons, Apostles' Creeds, a voyage of Peter Simon to Rome, a combat of miracles between this Simon and another Simon, a so-called magician. In a word: there is not a trick, a fraud, an imposture, that the Nazarenes do not bring into play: and after that they tell us calmly that the so-called apostles could not have been deceived nor deceivers, and that one must believe witnesses who had their throat cut to give weight to their testimony.

O miserable deceivers and deceived who talk like this! what proof do you have that these apostles wrote what has been put over their name? If it was possible to make up canons, could one not make up gospels? Do you not yourselves recognize forgeries? Who told you that the apostles died to give weight to their testimony? There is not a single contemporary historian who even mentions Jesus and his apostles. Admit that you support lies by lies; admit that the rage of dominating men's minds, fanaticism, and the passage of time, have established this edifice that is today crumbling on all sides—a ruin detested by reason and sustained by error.

After three hundred years, they succeeded in having this Jesus acknowledged as a god; and, not content with this blasphemy, they push their extravagance even farther by putting this god into a piece of dough; and, while their god is eaten by mice, digested, expelled with excrement, they maintain that there is no bread in their host, that it is God alone who has taken the place of the bread, at the command of a man. All superstitions come in crowds to inundate the Church; rapine presides over it; they sell remission of sins, they sell indulgences as much as benefices, and everything is up for auction.

This sect divides itself into a multitude of sects: at all times they battle, murder each other, slit each others' throats. In every dispute kings and princes are murdered.

This, my very dear brethren, is the fruit of the tree of the cross of the gibbet which they deified.

This, then, was the reason they dared to have God come to earth! To deliver Europe over to murder and brigandage for centuries. It is true that our fathers have cast off a part of this frightful yoke; that they have got rid of several errors, several superstitions; but, good God, people have left their work incomplete! Everything indicates to us that the time has come to be done with it, and to destroy root and branch the idol of which we have barely broken some fingers. A crowd of theologians has already embraced Socinianism, which closely approaches the worship of a single God, free from superstition. England, Germany, our provinces, are full of wise doctors who only want to burst forth! And there is a large number of them, too, in other countries. Why then wait any longer? Why not worship God in spirit and in truth? Why obstinately continue to teach what we do not believe, and make ourselves guilty of an enormous crime before God?

We are told that the common people need mysteries, that they must be deceived. Ah, my brethren, can we commit this outrage on mankind? Have our fathers not already freed the people from transubstantiation, the worship of creatures and the bones of the dead, auricular confession, indulgences, exorcisms, false miracles and ridiculous images? Are the people not used to being deprived of such superstitious foods? We must have the courage to go a few steps farther; the common people is not as idiotic as many think; it will accept without difficulty a wise and simple creed of a single God, such as (they tell us) Abraham and Noah worshipped, such as all the sages of antiquity worshipped, such as is accepted in China by all literate men. We do not claim to deprive the priests of that which the liberality of the nations has bestowed on them; but we want these priests, who nearly all secretly ridicule the lies they retail, to join us in preaching the truth. Let them watch out: they offend the Divinity and dishonor it, and instead should glorify it. What inestimable good would be produced by such a happy change! Princes and magistrates would be obeyed more readily, people would be more peaceful, the spirit of division and hatred would be dissipated. One would offer God, in peace, the first-fruits of one's labor; there would certainly be more honesty in the world, for a large number of weak-minded persons who hear contemptuous talk every day about this Christian superstition, who know that it is ridiculed by the very priests themselves, imagine, without thinking, that actually there is no true religion—and they surrender themselves to a life of excess. But when they will know that the Christian sect is actually nothing more than the perversion of natural religion; when reason, freed from its chains, will teach the people that there is only one God, that this God is the universal father of all men, who are brothers; that these brothers must be good and just to one another, and that they must practice all the virtues; that God, being good and just, must reward virtue and punish crimes; surely, my brethren, men will be better for it, and less superstitious.

We are making a beginning by giving this example in secret, and we dare to hope that it will be followed in public.

May this great God who listens to me; this God who surely cannot have been born of a girl, nor died on the gibbet, nor be eaten in a piece of dough, nor have inspired these books, filled with contradictions, madness, and horror; may this God, creator of all the worlds, have pity on that sect of Christians that blasphemes him! May he lead them back to the holy and natural religion, and spread his blessings over our efforts to have him truly worshipped.   *Amen.*

Fragments*

Hermann Samuel Reimarus

The German religious situation was gravely complicated by divisions among, and sometimes within states. The crazy-quilt of German states was ruled by Lutheran, Calvinist, and Roman Catholic houses, and tolerance or persecution—more often the latter than the former—was strictly a local affair. But gradually a new spirit began to emerge, especially in Protestant northern Germany: there was a rebellion against the dry-as-dust pedantry of most pastors, against their orthodoxy uninformed by real learning and unleavened by true fervor. Pietists sought for a religion of the heart, liberal and well educated ministers began to read the Bible critically if devoutly, and enlightened philosophers like Christian Thomasius and Christian Wolff taught a benevolent deity, a rational universe, and the need for mutual tolerance.

It was in this atmosphere that deism slowly, timidly, grew in Germany. Its most remarkable representative was Hermann Samuel Reimarus (1694-1768), a teacher in Hamburg, who had in a lifetime of private torment stripped off all remnants of Christian belief. This was not known until after his death, when the great German critic and playwright Lessing got access to a large unpublished manuscript of Reimarus', the fruit of long and anxious labor, the Apologie oder Schutzschrift für die vernünftigen Verehrer Gottes. *Fascinated by a book that expressed so many of his own convictions, Lessing published a series of fragments from it between 1774 and 1778, the so-called* Wolfenbüttel Fragments, *without naming their author. These fragments, in brief, assert the following: the pure simple teaching of Jesus has been corrupted by priests, but the true Christian is he who follows Jesus rather than the priests; clerics do wrong to decry reason from their pulpits: since reason is the only method*

* I have taken this fragment from Lessing's transcription, in Lessing, *Sämmtliche Schriften*, ed. Karl Lachmann and Franz Muncker, XII (1897), 359-368 *passim*. Translation by Peter Gay.

159

of discovering the true deity, reason should be cultivated rather than disparaged; for God made a regular and perfect natural order, miracles would be contradictory of his power, disturbing his work, and revelations are therefore redundant; the Old Testament is filled with difficulties—witness as only one instance the passage of the Children of Israel through the Red Sea; it is not probable that the Old Testament was designed to reveal to man the truths of divine religion: after all, it says nothing about the immortality of the soul, and it is this very doctrine that all natural religion acknowledges as true; the evangelists contradict one another, and fatally so, about the resurrection story.

Except for the first of these, published in 1774, Lessing brought out these fragments in 1777, and aroused vehement controversy. Undaunted, he returned in the following year with another long fragment which portrays Jesus as a parochial leader of the Jews who had cared for his people only, but whose limited program was expanded out of all recognition after his death by his fanatical followers. The Christian religion—not to put too fine a point on it—was simply a deception.

The consequences were inevitable. The Duke of Brunswick, who had exempted Lessing from the censorship, now reimposed it, and Lessing ceased publishing further fragments. Instead, he wrote his celebrated play, Nathan der Weise, a long parable preaching toleration. It was a noble epitaph to the deist controversy in Germany.

THIRD FRAGMENT: PASSAGE OF THE ISRAELITES THROUGH THE RED SEA

If we look at . . . the miracle of the passage through the Red Sea, its inner contradiction, its impossibility, is quite palpable. Six hundred thousand Israelites of military age leave Egypt, armed, and in battle order. They have with them their wives and their children and a good deal of rabble that had joined them. Now, we must count for each man of military age, four others at least; partly women, partly children, partly the aged, partly servants. The number of the emigrants, therefore, in proportion to those of military age, must be at least 3,000,000 souls. They take with them all their sheep and oxen, that is to say a large number of cattle. If we count only 300,000 heads of households, and give each of them one cow or ox and two sheep, that would add up to 300,000 oxen and cows, and 600,000 sheep and goats. In addition, we must count on at least 1,000 wagon loads of hay or fodder; to say nothing of the many other wagons containing the golden and silver vessels which they had purloined, and piles of baggage and tents needed for such an enormous army—even if we count only 5,000 wagons, which is one wagon to sixty persons. At least they arrived at the Red Sea, and put down their camp near its shore. Pharaoh followed them, with 600 selected wagons and all the wagons left in Egypt, in addition to all the cavalry and infantry, and, as it was nightfall, he settled down not far from them. Josephus estimates this army at 50,000 cavalrymen and 200,000 infantry. It cannot have been small, for it was planning to confront an army of 600,000. But let us only count half of this—namely 25,000 cavalrymen, and 100,000 infantry, plus the wagons. During the night, the column of cloud and fire places itself between the Israelites and the Egyptians; God then sends a strong easterly wind which through the whole night pushes away the sea and makes the ground dry. Then the Isrealites enter, dry of foot, and the Egyptians follow them, so that the former have crossed while the latter are in the middle of the sea. In the watch of the morning, God looks down upon the army of the Egyptians, allows the water to return so that it is restored to its full flood, and thus all the Egyptians drown, and not a one remains. It is this that the Biblical narrative partly tells us explicitly, partly compels us to infer.

I shall here set aside all other circumstances, and consider only the fantastic march in comparison to the short time, to the mass of men and beasts, to the inconvenient road and the dark night. As the easterly wind had been blowing all night to dry the sea, it cannot have been dry before midnight. Now, in the watch of the morning—that is, after three in the morning—the Egyptians are already in the middle of the sea, with horse and baggage. Then, toward morning, the water returns: the Egyptians flee back, but run into the water and drown. It follows that in the time between midnight and three or four in the morning, not merely all Israelites had marched through the sea to the other shore, but also all the Egyptians had marched to the middle of the sea. Whoever has, I will not even say, marched with an army, but even read or heard of one, can easily understand that such a quick flight is a complete impossibility, especially considering the quantity of men and beasts, and all the attendant circumstances. The men add up to 3,100,000; then the Israelites have 6,000 wagons with fodder and baggage, drawn by the above-mentioned oxen. The Egyptians had a large number of military wagons, equipped with two, four, or perhaps more horses—at least, with the cavalry, 100,000 horses. Add the cattle of the Israelites: 300,000 oxen and cows, and 600,000 sheep. When such an enormous number of men and cattle sets up a camp, it would need a space of many square miles; we learn this not merely from our contemporary experience, but from the ancient manner of camping. The camp of the Hebrews, as we can see from the meeting tent and the cities of the Levites, was square. And it is logical that an army waiting for a hostile assault would not spread itself out lengthwise and thus weaken itself, but would be kept together. A square would therefore be most convenient; and indeed, the Romans and other nations liked square camps. Now even if we put 10 persons in each tent, the number of 3,000,000 persons gives us 300,000 tents. And they would be put into a square, but taking into the center the baggage, the wagons, and the cattle, for their protection. Now if we consider the enormous space required by 300,000 oxen, 600,000 sheep, and thousands of baggage wagons, and how far 300,000 tents would have to extend around them; then we say very little if we claim that no matter how cleverly it was all arranged, the whole must cover more than two German square miles. Now, since there would have to be a great distance between the army of the Israelites and the Egyptians, it is further obvious that we are not exaggerating when we say that the nearest Egyptian would have to be at least a mile from the Israelites—that is to say, three miles from the sea. The sea itself, if we measure it in accord with the narrative, must have been at least a German mile wide, considering that Pharaoh's whole army, with so many horses and wagons, found, all at once, room and its grave in it. So that the nearest Egyptians must have been at least four German miles from the place in which they drowned, and the last of the Israelites too must have been about four German miles from that spot in the Red Sea.

Now one might think that it is not really impossible to march four miles in four hours. However, if one is used to visualizing matters with all their circumstances with any clarity, and especially if one knows the habits of Orientals and the bottom of the sea, then one will have no trouble recognizing that such a march —four German miles long, in four hours, across the bottom of the sea permitting passage to only a few at a time—would be an absolute impossibility [etc., etc.].

D. AMERICAN DEISM

READING NO. 9

The Age of Reason*

Thomas Paine

When Thomas Paine described The Age of Reason (*from which an excerpt follows*) *as "the last offering" he would make to his "fellow citizens of all nations," he was dangerously near speaking the truth. At the time he submitted the manuscript for publication he was under sentence of death by guillotine. But then, after the overthrow of the Jacobins (whom he had angered, by opposing, among other things, the execution of Louis XVI), he was released and completed the remaining two parts of* The Age of Reason.

By the time he came to write this summary of deist belief, he was already famous. He had achieved his first fame with his tract Common Sense, *and the* American Crisis *papers, designed to bolster the Colonists' morale in their struggle for independence. After the American Revolution, he continued his pamphleteering in England; but his* Rights of Man, *written in defense of the French Revolution and against Burke's enormously effective antirevolutionary* Reflections on the Revolution in France (1790), *aroused the displeasure of the government and led to his indictment for treason, which he escaped by fleeing to Revolutionary France.*

Theodore Roosevelt described this restless revolutionary as a "filthy little atheist," but he was neither filthy nor little nor an atheist. He was hated in part because he was a brilliant stylist—the sentence "these are the times that try men's souls" is characteristic of his economy, clarity, and effectiveness—and an un-

* The Age of Reason, Being an Investigation of Time and Fabulous Theology, from Vol. 5, The Life and Writings of Thomas Paine, Vincent Parke and Company, New York, 1908.

sparing controversialist. But he was a religious man. Mixing his Quaker upbringing with his rationalism, he defended a beneficent deity and natural religion based on reason. He was, in a word, the last of the deists.

It has been my intention, for several years past, to publish my thoughts upon religion. I am well aware of the difficulties that attend the subject and, from that consideration, had reserved it to a more advanced period of life. I intended it to be the last offering I should make to my fellow citizens of all nations, and that at a time when the purity of the motive that induced me to it could not admit of a question, even by those who might disapprove the work.

The circumstance that has now taken place in France of the total abolition of the whole national order of priesthood, and of everything appertaining to compulsive systems of religion, and compulsive articles of faith, has not only precipitated my intention, but rendered a work of this kind exceedingly necessary, lest in the general wreck of superstition, of false systems of government and false theology, we lose sight of morality, of humanity, and of the theology that is true.

As several of my colleagues, and others of my fellow citizens of France, have given me the example of making their voluntary and individual profession of faith, I also will make mine; and I do this with all that sincerity and frankness with which the mind of man communicates with itself.

I believe in one God, and no more; and I hope for happiness beyond this life.

I believe in the equality of man; and I believe that religious duties consist in doing justice, loving mercy, and endeavoring to make our fellow creatures happy.

But, lest it should be supposed that I believe in many other things in addition to these, I shall, in the progress of this work, declare the things I do not believe, and my reasons for not believing them.

I do not believe in the creed professed by the Jewish church, by the Roman church, by the Greek church, by the Turkish church, by the Protestant church, nor by any church that I know of. My own mind is my own church.

All national institutions of churches, whether Jewish, Christian, or Turkish, appear to me no other than human inventions, set up to terrify and enslave mankind, and monopolize power and profit.

I do not mean by this declaration to condemn those who believe otherwise; they have the same right to their belief as I have to mine. But it is necessary to the happiness of man that he be mentally faithful to himself. Infidelity does not consist in believing or in disbelieving; it consists in professing to believe what he does not believe.

It is impossible to calculate the moral mischief, if I may so express it, that mental lying has produced in society. When a man has so far corrupted and prostituted the chastity of his mind as to subscribe his professional belief to things he does not believe, he has prepared himself for the commission of every other crime. He takes up the trade of a priest for the sake of gain, and in order to qualify himself for that trade he begins with a perjury. Can we conceive anything more destructive to morality than this?

Soon after I had published the pamphlet *Common Sense* in America, I saw the exceeding probability that a revolution in the system of government would be followed by a revolution in the system of religion. The adulterous connection of church and state, wherever it had taken place, whether Jewish, Christian, or Turkish, had so effectually prohibited, by pains and penalties, every discussion upon established creeds and upon first principles of religion that, until the system of government should be changed, those subjects could not be brought fairly and openly before the world; but that, whenever this should be done, a revolution in the system of religion would follow. Human inventions and priestcraft would be detected, and man would return to the pure, unmixed, and unadulterated belief of one God, and no more.

Every national church or religion has established itself by pretending some special mission from God, communicated to certain individuals. The Jews have their Moses; the Christians their Jesus Christ, their apostles and saints; and the Turks their Mohammed, as if the way to God was not open to every man alike.

Each of those churches show certain books which they call "revelation," or the word of God. The Jews say that their word of God was given by God to Moses, face to face; the Christians say their word of God came by divine inspiration; and the Turks say that their word of God (the Koran) was brought by an angel from heaven. Each of those churches accuse the other of unbelief; and for my part I disbelieve them all.

As it is necessary to affix right ideas to words, I will, before I proceed further into the subject, offer some observations on the word "revelation." Revelation, when applied to religion, means something communicated *immediately* from God to man.

No one will deny or dispute the power of the Almighty to make such a communication, if he pleases. But admitting, for the sake of a case, that something has been revealed to a certain person, and not revealed to any other person, it is revelation to that person only. When he tells it to a second person, a second to a third, a third to a fourth, and so on, it ceases to be a revelation to all those persons. It is revelation to the first person only, and *hearsay* to every other, and consequently they are not obliged to believe it.

It is a contradiction in terms and ideas to call anything a revelation that comes to us at second hand, either verbally or in writing. Revelation is necessarily limited to the first communication—after this, it is only an account of something which that person says was a revelation made to him; and though he may find himself obliged to believe it, it cannot be incumbent on me to believe it in the same manner, for it was not a revelation made to *me,* and I have only his word for it that it was made to him.

When Moses told the children of Israel that he received the two tables of the Commandments from the hands of God, they were not obliged to believe him, because they had no other authority for it than his telling them so; and I have no other authority for it than some historian telling me so. The Commandments carry no internal evidence of divinity with them; they contain some good moral precepts, such as any man qualified to be a lawgiver, or a legislator, could produce himself without having recourse to supernatural intervention.[1]

---

[1] It is, however, necessary to except the declaration which says that God *visits the sins of the fathers upon the children;* it is contrary to every principle of moral justice.

When I am told that the Koran was written in heaven and brought to Mohammed by an angel, the account comes too near the same kind of hearsay evidence and secondhand authority as the former. I did not see the angel myself, and therefore I have a right not to believe it.

When also I am told that a woman called the Virgin Mary said, or gave out, that she was with child without any cohabitation with a man, and that her betrothed husband, Joseph, said that an angel told him so, I have a right to believe them or not; such a circumstance required a much stronger evidence than their bare word for it; but we have not even this—for neither Joseph nor Mary wrote any such matter themselves; it is only reported by other that *they said so*—it is hearsay upon hearsay, and I do not choose to rest my belief upon such evidence.

It is, however, not difficult to account for the credit that was given to the story of Jesus Christ being the son of God. He was born when the heathen mythology had still some fashion and repute in the world, and that mythology had prepared the people for the belief of such a story. Almost all the extraordinary men that lived under the heathen mythology were reputed to be the sons of some of their gods. It was not a new thing, at that time, to believe a man to have been celestially begotten; the intercourse of gods with women was then a matter of familiar opinion. Their Jupiter, according to their accounts, had cohabited with hundreds: the story, therefore, had nothing in it either new, wonderful, or obscene; it was conformable to the opinions that then prevailed among the people called Gentiles or mythologists, and it was those people only that believed it. The Jews who had kept strictly to the belief of one God, and no more, and who had always rejected the heathen mythology, never credited the story.

It is curious to observe how the theory of what is called the Christian church sprung out of the tail of the heathen mythology. A direct incorporation took place in the first instance, by making the reputed founder to be celestially begotten. The trinity of gods that then followed was no other than a reduction of the former plurality, which was about twenty or thirty thousand; the statue of Mary succeeded the statue of Diana of Ephesus; the deification of heroes changed into the canonization of saints; the mythologists had gods for everything; the Christian mythologists had saints for everything; the church became as crowded with one, as the Pantheon had been with the other, and Rome was the place of both. The Christian theory is little else than the idolatry of the ancient mythologists accommodated to the purpose of power and revenue, and it yet remains to reason and philosophy to abolish the amphibious fraud.

Nothing that is here said can apply, even with the most distant disrespect, to the real character of Jesus Christ. He was a virtuous and an amiable man. The morality that he preached and practiced was of the most benevolent kind; and though similar systems of morality had been preached by Confucius and by some of the Greek philosophers many years before, by the Quakers since, and by many good men in all ages, it has not been exceeded by any.

Jesus Christ wrote no account of himself, of his birth, parentage, or anything else; not a line of what is called the New Testament is of his own writing. The history of him is altogether the work of other people; and as to the account of his resurrection and ascension, it was the necessary counterpart to the story of his birth. His historians, having brought him into the world in a supernatural manner, were obliged to take him out again in the same manner, or the first part of the story must have fallen to the ground.

The wretched contrivance with which the latter part is told exceeds everything that went before it. The first part, that of the miraculous conception, was not a thing that admitted of publicity; and therefore the tellers of this part of the story had this advantage that, though they might not be credited, they could not be detected. They could not be expected to prove it because it was not one of those things that admitted of proof, and it was impossible that the person of whom it was told could prove it himself.

But the resurrection of a dead person from the grave, and his ascension through the air, is a thing very different, as to the evidence it admits of, to the invisible conception of a child in the womb. The resurrection and ascension, supposing them to have taken place, admitted of public and ocular demonstration, like that of the ascension of a balloon or the sun at noonday, to all

Jerusalem at least. A thing which everybody is required to believe requires that the proof and evidence of it should be equal to all and universal; and as the public visibility of this last related act was the only evidence that could give sanction to the former part, the whole of it falls to the ground because that evidence never was given. Instead of this, a small number of persons, not more than eight or nine, are introduced as proxies for the whole world, to say they saw it, and all the rest of the world are called upon to believe it. But it appears that Thomas did not believe the resurrection and, as they say, would not believe without having ocular and manual demonstration himself. *So neither will I,* and the reason is equally as good for me and for every other person as for Thomas.

It is in vain to attempt to palliate or disguise this matter. The story, so far as relates to the supernatural part, has every mark of fraud and imposition stamped upon the face of it. Who were the authors of it is as impossible for us now to know, as it is for us to be assured that the books in which the account is related were written by the persons whose names they bear; the best surviving evidence we now have respecting this affair is the Jews. They are regularly descended from the people who lived in the times this resurrection and ascension is said to have happened, and they say *it is not true.* It has long appeared to me a strange inconsistency to cite the Jews as a proof of the truth of the story. It is just the same as if a man were to say, I will prove the truth of what I have told you by producing the people who say it is false.

That such a person as Jesus Christ existed, and that he was crucified, which was the mode of execution at that day, are historical relations strictly within the limits of probability. He preached most excellent morality and the equality of man, but he preached also against the corruptions and avarice of the Jewish priests, and this brought upon him the hatred and vengeance of the whole order of priesthood. The accusation which those priests brought against him was that of sedition and conspiracy against the Roman government, to which the Jews were then subject and tributary; and it is not improbable that the Roman government might have some secret apprehensions of the effects of his doctrine, as well as the Jewish priests; neither is it improbable that Jesus Christ had in contemplation the delivery of the Jewish nation from the bondage of the Romans. Between the two, however, this virtuous reformer and revolutionist lost his life.

It is upon this plain narrative of facts, together with another case I am going to mention, that the Christian mythologists, calling themselves the Christian church, have erected their fable which, for absurdity and extravagance, is not exceeded by anything that is to be found in the mythology of the ancients.

The ancient mythologists tell us that the race of Giants made war against Jupiter, and that one of them threw a hundred rocks against him at one throw; that Jupiter defeated him with thunder, and confined him afterward under Mount Etna, and that every time the Giant turns himself Mount Etna belches fire.

It is here easy to see that the circumstance of the mountain, that of its being a volcano, suggested the idea of the fable; and that the fable is made to fit and wind itself up with that circumstance.

The Christian mytholgists tell us that their Satan made war against the Almighty, who defeated him and confined him afterward, not under a mountain, but in a pit. It is here easy to see that the first fable suggested the idea of the second; for the fable of Jupiter and the Giants was told many hundred years before that of Satan.

Thus far the ancient and the Christian mythologists differ very little from each other. But the latter have contrived to carry the matter much farther. They have contrived to connect the fabulous part of the story of Jesus Christ with the fable originating from Mount Etna; and in order to make all the parts of the story tie together, they have taken to their aid the traditions of the Jews; for the Christian mythology is made up partly from the ancient mythology and partly from the Jewish traditions.

The Christian mythologists, after having confined Satan in a pit, were obliged to let him out again to bring on the sequel of the fable. He is then introduced into the Garden of Eden in the shape of a snake or a serpent, and in that shape he enters into familiar conversation with Eve, who is noway surprised to hear a snake talk; and the issue of this *tête-à-tête* is that he persuades her to eat an apple, and the eating of that apple damns all mankind.

After giving Satan this triumph over the whole creation, one would have supposed that the church mythologists would have been kind enough to send him back again to the pit; or, if they had not done this, that they would have put a mountain upon him (for they say that their faith can remove a mountain), or have put him *under* a mountain, as the former mythologists had done, to prevent him getting again among the women and doing more mischief. But instead of this they leave him at large, without even obliging him to give his parole—the secret of which is that they could not do without him; and after being at the trouble of making him, they bribed him to stay. They promised him *all* the Jews, *all* the Turks by anticipation, nine-tenths of the world besides, and Mohammed into the bargain. After this, who can doubt the bountifulness of the Christian mythology?

Having thus made an insurrection and a battle in Heaven, in which none of the combatants could be either killed or wounded —put Satan into the pit—let him out again—giving him a triumph over the whole creation—damned all mankind by the eating of an apple, these Christian mythologists bring the two ends of their fable together. They represent this virtuous and amiable man, Jesus Christ, to be at once both God and man, and also the Son of God, celestially begotten, on purpose to be sacrificed, because they say that Eve in her longing had eaten an apple.

Putting aside everything that might excite laughter by its absurdity, or detestation by its profaneness, and confining ourselves merely to an examination of the parts, it is impossible to conceive a story more derogatory to the Almighty, more inconsistent with his wisdom, more contradictory to his power than this story is.

In order to make for it a foundation to rise upon, the inventors were under the necessity of giving to the being whom they call Satan a power equally as great, if not greater, than they attribute to the Almighty. They have not only given him the power of liberating himself from the pit, after what they call his fall, but they have made that power increase afterward to infinity. Before this fall they represent him only as an angel of limited existence, as they represent the rest. After his fall, he becomes, by their account, omnipresent. He exists everywhere, and at the same time. He occupies the whole immensity of space.

Not content with this deification of Satan, they represent him as defeating, by stratagem, in the shape of an animal of the creation, all the power and wisdom of the Almighty. They represent him as having compelled the Almighty to the *direct necessity* either of surrendering the whole of the creation to the government and sovereignty of this Satan or of capitulating for its redemption by coming down upon earth and exhibiting himself upon a cross in the shape of a man.

Had the inventors of this story told it the contrary way, that is, had they represented the Almighty as compelling Satan to exhibit *himself* on a cross, in the shape of a snake, as a punishment for his new transgression, the story would have been less absurd—less contradictory. But instead of this, they make the transgressor triumph, and the Almighty fall.

That many good men have believed this strange fable and lived very good lives under that belief (for credulity is not a crime) is what I have no doubt of. In the first place, they were educated to believe it, and they would have believed anything else in the same manner. There are also many who have been so enthusiastically enraptured by what they conceived to be the infinite love of God to man, in making a sacrifice himself, that the vehemence of the idea has forbidden and deterred them from examining into the absurdity and profaneness of the story. The more unnatural anything is, the more it is capable of becoming the object of dismal admiration.

But if objects for gratitude and admiration are our desire, do they not present themselves every hour to our eyes? Do we not see a fair creation prepared to receive us the instant we are born —a world furnished to our hands that cost us nothing? Is it we that light up the sun, that pour down the rain and fill the earth with abundance? Whether we sleep or wake, the vast machinery of the universe still goes on. Are these things, and the blessings they indicate in future, nothing to us? Can our gross feelings be excited by no other subjects than tragedy and suicide? Or is the gloomy pride of man become so intolerable that nothing can flatter it but a sacrifice of the Creator?

I know that this bold investigation will alarm many, but it

would be paying too great a compliment to their credulity to
forbear it on their account; the times and the subject demand it
to be done. The suspicion that the theory of what is called the
Christian church is fabulous is becoming very extensive in all
countries; and it will be a consolation to men staggering under
that suspicion, and doubting what to believe and what to disbelieve, to see the object freely investigated. I therefore pass
on to the examinations of the books called the Old and New
Testament.

These books, beginning with Genesis and ending with Revelation (which by the by, is a book of riddles that requires a revelation to explain it), are, we are told, the word of God. It is,
therefore, proper for us to know who told us so, that we may
know what credit to give to the report. The answer to this question is that nobody can tell, except that we tell one another so.
The case, however, historically appears to be as follows:

When the church mythologists established their system, they
collected all the writings they could find and managed them as
they pleased. It is a matter altogether of uncertainty to us
whether such of the writings as now appear under the name of
the Old and New Testament are in the same state in which
those collectors say they found them, or whether they added,
altered, abridged, or dressed them up.

Be this as it may, they decided by *vote* which of the books out
of the collection they had made should be the *word of God,* and
which should not. They rejected several; they voted others to
be doubtful, such as the books called the Apocrypha; and those
books which had a majority of votes were voted to be the word
of God. Had they voted otherwise, all the people, since calling
themselves Christians, had believed otherwise—for the belief of
the one comes from the vote of the other. Who the people were
that did all this we know nothing of; they called themselves by
the general name of the Church, and this is all we know of the
matter.

As we have no other external evidence or authority for believing these books to be the word of God than what I have
mentioned, which is no evidence or authority at all, I come, in
the next place, to examine the internal evidence contained in
the books themselves.

In the former part of this essay I have spoken of revelation; I now proceed further with that subject, for the purpose of applying it to the books in question.

Revelation is a communication of something which the person to whom that thing is revealed did not know before. For if I have done a thing or seen it done, it needs no revelation to tell me I have done it or seen it, nor to enable me to tell it or to write it.

Revelation, therefore, cannot be applied to anything done upon earth, of which man himself is the actor or the witness; and, consequently, all the historical and anecdotal parts of the Bible, which is almost the whole of it, is not within the meaning and compass of the word "revelation," and, therefore, is not the word of God.

When Samson ran off with the gateposts of Gaza, if he ever did so (and whether he did or not is nothing to us), or when he visited his Delilah, or caught his foxes, or did anything else, what has revelation to do with these things? If they were facts, he could tell them himself, or his secretary, if he kept one, could write them if they were worth either telling or writing; and if they were fictions, revelation could not make them true; and whether true or not, we are neither the better nor the wiser for knowing them. When we contemplate the immensity of that Being who directs and governs the incomprehensible *whole* of which the utmost ken of human sight can discover but a part, we ought to feel shame at calling such paltry stories the word of God.

As to the account of the Creation, with which the Book of Genesis opens, it has all the appearance of being a tradition which the Israelites had among them before they came into Egypt; and after their departure from that country they put it at the head of their history, without telling (as it is most probable) that they did not know how they came by it. The manner in which the account opens shows it to be traditionary. It begins abruptly; it is nobody that speaks; it is nobody that hears; it is addressed to nobody; it has neither first, second, nor third person; it has every criterion of being a tradition; it has no voucher. Moses does not take it upon himself by introducing it with the

formality that he uses on other occasions, such as that of saying,
"The Lord spake unto Moses, saying. . . ."

Why it has been called the Mosaic account of the Creation,
I am at a loss to conceive. Moses, I believe, was too good a judge
of such subjects to put his name to that account. He had been
educated among the Egyptians, who were a people as well
skilled in science and particularly in astronomy as any people
of their day; and the silence and caution that Moses observes in
not authenticating the account is a good negative evidence that
he neither told it nor believed it. The case is that every nation
of people has been worldmakers, and the Israelites had as much
right to set up the trade of worldmaking as any of the rest; and
as Moses was not an Israelite, he might not choose to contradict
the tradition. The account, however, is harmless; and this is
more than can be said of many other parts of the Bible.

Whenever we read the obscene stories, the voluptuous de-
baucheries, the cruel and torturous executions, the unrelenting
vindictiveness, with which more than half the Bible is filled, it
would be more consistent that we called it the word of a demon
than the word of God. It is a history of wickedness that has
served to corrupt and brutalize mankind; and, for my part, I
sincerely detest it, as I detest everything that is cruel.

We scarcely meet with anything, a few phrases excepted, but
what deserves either our abhorrence or our contempt, till we
come to the miscellaneous parts of the Bible. In the anonymous
publications, the Psalms and the Book of Job, more particularly
in the latter, we find a great deal of elevated sentiment rever-
entially expressed of the power and benignity of the Almighty;
but they stand on no higher rank than many other compositions
on similar subjects, as well before that time as since. . . .

Principles of Nature*

Elihu Palmer

While the celebrity of Tom Paine has remained constant, and Elihu Palmer is remembered by the specialist alone, it was Palmer rather than Paine who wrote the "Bible" of American Deism with his Principles of Nature. *It was the* Principles *that furnished texts for readings at meetings of Deist societies. The excerpts that follow are therefore fitting for a close of a collection of deist writings.*

Elihu Palmer began as a Baptist clergyman, but he was driven from his pulpit—properly enough—for denying, and preaching against, the divinity of Christ. Palmer claimed that he had arrived at his deist conviction that the Christian religion was neither divine nor true in the service of true Christianity, but others did not see it his way, and sent him into the wilderness of secular life.

After abandoning the cloth, Palmer took up the practice of law, but his career at the bar was cut short by an attack of yellow fever, incurred during one of those epidemics that cursed the early years of the Republic, and left him widowed, blind, and unable to continue in the legal profession. It was then that he turned his considerable talents to the cause of deism, organizing deist societies, writing their constitutions, devising their ritual, and editing deist journals.

His most remarkable effort is Principles of Nature. *While he apologizes, in the Preface, for faults of grammar and style due to the difficulties of writing in blindness, he made no apologies*

---

* Principles of Nature, or A Development of the Moral Causes of *Happiness and Misery among the Human Species*, by R. Carlile, London, 1823, pp. 173-180, 201-206.

for his ideas, and for his effort to divorce morality from theology. Nor did he need to apologize.

MORAL PRINCIPLE.

In the sacred writings of the Jews and Christians in all ancient and theological compositions, the idea of correct and moral principle had been so frequently abandoned, and so grossly violated, that the energy of thought, for many ages, was inadequate to an upright and full investigation of the nature of human actions. The subject is no doubt, connected with considerable difficulties; but these difficulties have been essentially augmented by the rubbish with which superstition has covered the moral character of man. The proofs of any inquiry, which relate to moral principle, adhere so closely to the realities of physical and intellectual existence, that the errors of an upright and intelligent mind can never assume a frightful and destructive character. They will be continually modified, and undergo frequent corrections by the new information of which the mind is continually susceptible.

Moral science cannot, perhaps, be reduced to absolute certitude, or become susceptible of absolute perfection; it is in its nature progressive, and the infinite diversity of sensations, which constitute the essential basis of all our intellectual combinations and deductions, will furnish, at least, a suspicion, that the decisions of the mind upon this subject ought frequently to be re-examined and subjected to a new and more accurate scrutiny. All the theological systems that ever have been written, have never thrown a particle of light upon this most interesting inquiry; they have established precepts, some few of which are good, and others extremely immoral; but no anlysis of the physical or moral powers of man has ever been exhibited; no developement of the principles of causation, or the nature of those effects, which have essentially resulted from the constitution of animal or intellectual existence. In all these cases, supernatural theology has prudently observed an absolute silence, probably from a consciousness of the most profound ignorance. This single truth, of itself, evinces the moral deficiency of supernatural religion, and the necessity of returning to the basis of nature for a correct developement of principle. Every thing that is discordant to this has been established by the force of authority, and the reasonableness of such establishment has never been a ground of serious enquiry.

If it should be objected, that it is impossible, even upon the basis of nature, to find an universal standard of morality, it will nevertheless appear, that a continual approach toward such a standard must be far preferable to those arbitrary decisions which theology has made upon this subject. There can be no internal force or excellence connected with a system established solely by external power, without reference to the essence or character of the principles which constitute the body of such a system. The internal excellence of the principle itself, together with capacity of mental discernment, is essential to the ultimate benefit which may be expected from the natural operation of legal codes. But there is no better method of rendering a principle intelligible than by shewing that it is consistent with nature, that it has resulted from her laws that it is useful in its effect, that it is capable of being reduced to practice; in a word, that it is suited to the powers, conditions, and character of the human species.

There is another previous consideration also, which ought to be taken into the account before we shall be able to comprehend the essence of moral principle, or to understand the nature of those duties which result from our original constitutions. That intellectual part of man, which supernatural theology has denominated a soul, has been viewed seperate and distinct from the body, as a kind of spiritual and celestial inhabitant of a mean and material tenement; that their union would be of short duration, and that their final destination was extremely different. This led to reasonings and conjectures that were erroneous; for as the corporeal sensations were entirely excluded from a participation in the cause, by which moral influence was produced, an accurate knowledge of the sources of action was necessarily excluded, and spiritual mystery was substituted for philosophic demonstration.

The human mind is incapable of forming any conception of that which is not material; man is a being whose composition is purely physical, and moral properties or intellect are the necessary results of organic construction. To ascertain, therefore, the foundation of moral principle, it is necessary to revert to the physical constitution of human nature, it is necessary to go to the source of sensation, to the cause of impressions, and the diversity of these impressions; to the universality of the fact, that all human nature possesses the same or similar sensations, together with all the other additional circumstances resulting from the subsequent intellectual combinations of our existence. All human beings are susceptible of pain, they are also all susceptible of pleasure; they are all possessed of the same senses, subjected to the same wants, exhibit the same desires, and are satisfied with the same enjoyments. These positions cannot be controverted, they are true in the general features of their character and the inconsiderable deviations resulting from the variations of animal structure, cannot in any eminent degree, shake the rectitude or universality of these positions. The modification of the principle of animal structures in intelligent existence, is, no doubt, diversified by a nice and inscrutable gradation, but the aggregate amount of organic result must be nearly the same, and though the animal sensation were to vary in a still higher degree, yet it would nevertheless, be substantially true, that certain comprehensive axioms might be laid down, which would necessarily include within the sphere of their imperious effect, every possible diversification of the sensitive faculties of human nature.

That happiness is to be preferred to misery, pleasure to pain, virtue to vice, truth to falsehood, science to ignorance, order to confusion, universal good to universal evil, are positions which no rational being can possibly controvert. They are positions to which mankind, in all ages and countries, must yield assent. They are positions, the truth of which is never denied, the essence of which is never controverted; it is the form and application only which has been the cause of social contention, and not the reality or excellence of the axioms themselves.

The universality of the principle of sensation gene rates universal capacity of enjoying pleasure and suffering pain; this circumstance modifies the character of human actions, and renders it necessary that every man should regard every other man with an eye of strict justice, with a tender and delicate sensibility, with a constant reference to the preservation of his feelings, and the extension of his happiness; in a word, that the exercise of eternal justice should be constantly reciprocated by all the individuals of the same species. If I assume to myself the pretended right of injuring the sensations, the moral sentiments, or general happiness of my neighbour, he has, undoubtedly, an equal right to commit the same violence upon me; this would go to the destruction of all right, to the total subversion of all justice; it would reduce society instantly to a state of warfare, and introduce the reign of terror and misery.

It is a contradiction in terms to assert that any man has a right to do wrong; the exercise of such a pretended right is the absolute destruction of all right, and the first human being who commits violence, has already prepared for himself a hell of retaliation, the justice of which his own mind can never deny. It is, therefore, inconsistent with truth to say, that there is no such thing as a general standard of moral principle; this standard has a real existence in the construction of our nature; it is ascertained and regulated by the rule of reciprocal justice. It is absolute in the most important duties of human life; but in other cases of less weight and magnitude, it is discovered by the calculations of judgment, by the process of the understanding, and will sometimes vibrate between the impressions of sense and the subtle combinations which constitutes an ultimate moral decision.

If it be objected upon the suggestion of this idea, that the system of natural morality is less perfect than that which has been revealed, the true answer is, that revealed morality, in the most intelligible cases, is incorrect and absurd; and in the more refined cases of difficulty, a total ignorance is manifested; so that it is evident, upon the very face of the record, that the subject of moral principle, in its subtle discriminations, was never examined or understood by theological writers. The boasted maxim of the Christian religion, "All things whatsoever ye would that men should do to you, do ye even so to them," is incorrect in point of phraseology, and in point of principle does not exceed any of the moral writers of antiquity, who lived many hundred years before Jesus Christ. If this scriptural declaration means to establish the doctrine of reciprocal justice, it is incontrovertibly right; but the idea of placing the essence of virtue in the *wishes* of the human heart, is not very correct. It is very possible that one human being may desire another to do unto him many things which ought not to be done, and which are, in their own nature, improper or immoral. To say, therefore, that our desires should constitute the basis of moral decision, is a declaration not consistent with truth, and which, in many cases, would subvert the very essence of moral principle.

There is a fitness or suitableness in the thing itself, united with the consideration of the good or bad effect that would be produced, which ought to become the ground of uniform and universal judgment in the human mind. My neighbour may wish me to do unto him an act of serious and substantial injury, which being performed, ought to be returned to me in manner and form exactly the same; and thus, by an adherence to this maxim as it is now stated, a double injury would be produced, and the foundation of virtue be shaken to the centre. But waving any criticism of this kind, and giving to this scripture declaration the full extent of what is contended for, it is, nevertheless, no more than a plain maxim of justice, which had been known and practised, in a greater or less degree at all times and in all countries. All the local and unjust institutions of mankind in former ages have not destroyed the essential relation which man bears to man, nor have they been able wholly to efface a knowledge of those duties which result from these relations, and from the powers and principles of human existence.

The more the subject of moral principle is examined, the more it will appear that there are certain general features in it which the experience of man has partially recognized, and being fully developed and reduced to practice, would constitute a solid foundation for human felicity. The approach to such a standard of perfection will be gradual and slow, but it must nevertheless, from the very nature of man, be constant and certain. "The following," says Volney, "is conceived to be the primordial basis and physical origin of all justice and right; whatever be the active power, the moving cause that directs the universe, this power having given to all men the same organs, the same sensations, and the same wants, has thereby declared, that it has also given them the same rights to the use of its benefits, and that in the order of nature all men are equal. Secondly, inasmuch as this power has given to every man the ability of preserving and maintaining his own existence, it clearly follows, that all men are constituted independent of each other, that they are created free, that no man can be subject, and no man sovereign, but that all men are the unlimited pro-proprietors of their own persons. Equality, therefore, and liberty, are two essential attributes of man, two laws of the Divinity, nor less essential and immutable than the physical properties of inanimate nature. Again, from the principle that every man is the unlimited master of his own person, it follows that one inseparable condition in every contract and engagement is the free and voluntary consent of all the persons therein bound; further, because every individual is equal to every other individual, it follows that the balance of receipts and payments in political society ought to be rigorously in equilibrium with each other; so that from the idea of equality, immediately flows that other idea, equity and justice."

Again, the same author observes, that "there existed in the order of the universe, and in the physical constitution of man, eternal and immutable laws, which waited only his observance to render him happy. O men of different climes! look to the heavens that give you light, to the earth that nourishes you; since they present to you all the same gifts; since the power that directs their motion has bestowed on you the same life, the same organs, the same wants, has it not also given you the same right to the use of its benefits? Has it not hereby declared you to be all equal and free? What mortal then shall dare refuse to his fellow-creature that which is granted him by Nature? O nations, let us banish all tyranny and discord! Let us form one society, one vast family; and since mankind are all constituted alike, let there henceforth exist but one law, that of nature; one code, that of reason; one throne, that of justice; one altar, that of union."

The foregoing impressive sentiments of this celebrated writer disclose with clearness to the view of the human mind, the nature of moral principle and the foundation of all right and all virtue. It is the reciprocation of sensation, the mutuality of condition, of powers and wants, that constitute the immortal basis of justice, and lead to the establishment of rules, whose operation must ever be in strict coincidence with the happiness of the human species. The exceptions to those fundamental principles are so few, and so unimportant, as to form no strong objection against the general assertion, that there exist in the constitution of human nature those essential properties which confer upon man the character of moral agent. To controvert, therefore, the existence of these moral principles, or the idea of a general standard in the morality of human actions, is to fly in the face of all experience, to oppose the universal consciousness of the human understanding, and deny the most conspicuous facts connected with the life of man. . . .

PHILOSOPHICAL IMMORTALITY.

"See matter next, with various life endued,
Press to one centre still, the general good.
See dying vegetables life sustain,
See life dissolving vegetate again:
All forms that perish other forms supply,
By turns we catch the vital breath and die.
Like bubbles on the sea of matter borne,
They rise, they break, and to that sea return."
—Pope's Essay on Man

The subject of a future life, has, in every age and country, in a greater or less degree, engaged the attention of man. That strong sentiment by which we are attached to life, has given to human sensations a most powerful impulse, and induced us to overleap the boundaries of the visible world, and seek in unknown or non-existent countries, the continuation of that existence which experience taught us it was necessary to abandon here.

The diversity of opinion which has prevailed upon this subject shews the difficulties which in some measure are essentially connected with the nature of the inquiry. The strong and active impulse which binds man to his personal identity has led to extravagant conceptions concerning the means of his preservation, and the new modes of existence, which, in the succession of ages, he imagined he was destined to experience. Religious fanaticism has indulged itself in the most ungarded manner, and enlisted heaven, earth, and hell, on its side, the better to accomplish its purposes; while philosophy, disgusted with the wild vagaries which religious imposture every where presented, seemed to incline to the opposite extreme. A contest commenced which has not yet terminated, and which presented alternately to the hopes and fears of man, the means of satisfying the one, and of destroying the other. Real consolation, however, was not furnished to the human mind by the virulence of their diversified discussions. It was to be expected in a case embarrassed with so many difficulties, that speculations would be endless, and decisions extremely variant.

As it commonly happens that people see more ghosts and spectres in the dark than in the light; so in the present case, the eagle eye of Superstition saw, or pretended to see, in the distant ages of futurity, and in the strange countries to which every intelligent being was hastening, all the peculiarities and local circumstances which would hereafter encircle the life of man. Thrones were erected, marble seats prepared, pomp and splendour in abundance, as the portion of that select company, whose ardent and fanatic hopes gave them a full assurance of a triumphant entry into the mansions of eternal glory; while, on the other hand, the hot, sulphurous, and infernal abodes, presented to the vicious and panic-struck mortal the dreadful considerations which stand connected with the idea of endless torture. Philosophy viewed the frantic ravings of religious enthusiasm with a mixed sentiment, composed of compassion and disgust. She sought in the constitution of nature for the discovery of some solid truths on which intelligent man might repose his existence, without fear and without trembling.

The progress of thought upon this subject has excited in superstitious minds the most rancorous sentiments of malignity; opprobrious epithets have been let out in abundance, merely because Reason laboured to discover, and declared that it had in some measure discovered, the real connection between man and nature. The terrific idea of annihilation still hovered around the dreaming abodes of fanaticism, and the most substantial and philosophic truth, which a knowledge of nature presented to man, became the ground of a most personal persecution and envenomed malice. Theology, however, frequently exhibits her weakness by condemning in others what might with great justice be charged to her own account.

If we advert for a moment to the sacred writings of the Jews and Christians, the folly of their high pretentions to a superior immortality will become very visible. The Old Testament furnishes no information relative to the subject of a future life. *Dust thou art, and unto dust thou shalt return; man has no pre-eminence above a beast, as the one dieth so dieth the other,* are phrases contained in the Old Testament; and are sweeping clauses against every hope of a future life, so far as such hope is founded upon this part of revealed religion; but it will be said, that the Gospel has brought life and immortality to light, and on this account rises in its claims to respect above the contemptible materialism of modern philosophy. It is true that the New Testament speaks of a future life; of Heaven and Hell; of the resurrection of the dead, &c. but it is necessary first to prove the truth of this part of the system before substantial deductions can be drawn in favour of any species of immortality. It is very easy to make naked and unsupported assertions, but unless the reason and evidence of the thing accompany these assertions, they are good for nothing. Paul, speaking of the human body, and of the resurrection of the dead, says, *It is sown a natural body, and it is raised a spiritual body;* by what kind of chymical process it is that matter is to become spirit, must be left to Paul and other spiritual chymists to determine.

The physical universe presents to the human understanding a grand and important spectacle of contemplation, in which the whole and the parts are essentially and indestructibly connected. There is no such thing as flying off in a spiritual or metaphysical tangent; every thing is bound by eternal laws to pass through the routine of its successive modes of existence, through the processive changes to which the laws of matter and motion have destined it.

There are two species of philosophical immortality; first, the immortality of matter, in its essential nature and character; and, secondly, the immortality of sensation in the aggregate mass of sensitive and intelligent life. These two perceptions must form the basis of every thing comprehensible upon this subject. The first needs no particular explanation, as the truth of the axiom, *that something can never become nothing,* is now generally admitted to be true; but the second idea ought to be rendered more intelligible. The opinions upon this subject have always supposed the existence of a spiritual, immaterial, and indestructible soul, which was capable of making its escape through the body, and passing in a light and airy manner through the atmospherical regions, spending an unconfined and uncontrollable existence in a manner inconceivable by our gross senses in their present condition.

The doctrine of transmigration is a branch of this system, and supposes that the souls of men may pass into other animals of an inferior kind, and reside there for a given time, by way of atonement for past crimes. These ideas of intellectual transmission, of solitary and distinct spirituality, are among those theological departures from philosophic truth which reason has to deplore, and which have retarded, in a very considerable degree, the progress of knowledge. It is in vain for man to deceive himself; a knowledge of his true condition in nature, and his relationship with all existence, will furnish a consolation far superior to all the theological reveries of antiquity. Matter is every where in motion; it is matter and motion, or the laws of the material world, by which innumerable sensitive and intelligent creatures are successively modified and disorganized. The rotation is eternal, and all the parts of nature may in time pass through the strictures of animal existence, and partake of the capacity of enjoying pleasure or suffering pain. In this warfare there is no discharge; an undying succession, an immortal mutation awaits the existence of every living creature. Nothing is durable in regard to modification or identity. In short, nothing is immortal but matter, its combinations and results; to wit, sensation and intellect.

But it is easy to perceive, that the continuation is specific and not personal; that man is destined to pass through an infinite diversity of predicaments, partaking at all times of the immortality essential to matter, and the perpetuated immortality of sensation in successive forms of animal existence. That this idea, so far from terrifying his mind, should furnish it with instructive lessons of sympathy, justice and universal benevolence.

If it should be objected here, that this is not the immortality to which man is so strongly attached, the answer is obvious, he must be reconciled to that kind of immortality, which nature prepares for her children, and which diffuses through the intelligent world a sentiment of equality, terrifying to every species of spiritual or political aristocracy.——It has frequently been said, that the ardent wishes of the human mind, in regard to immortal existence, furnish strong presumptive proof in favour of retrospect identity; but this error is visible upon the very face of the record. Thousands of individuals most ardently wish to continue their life here for ever; but this furnishes no barrier against the certain approach of death and final dissolution of the body. Human nature is accustomed to wish for more than it can obtain; its wishes, therefore, can never be brought as the standard of truth it might as well be expected that man should become immensely rich, because he wished to be so, as that he should immortalize his personal existence by the extent of his desires in this respect. It is true however, that whatever does exist must continue to exist for ever; this assertion regards substance and not forms; forms continually perish, but the essence of things is indestructible.

The ancient and orthodox idea is, that the[1] universe, with all its component parts, was made out of nothing; and if so, it must remain nothing, for it must be of the essence of which it was composed. It is a gross error to imagine that the eternal nature of things can be changed or destroyed by the operation of any power whatever. The great machinery of nature is governed by immutable laws; its motions are the result of its own internal energy. Hence it may be inferred that it is at once the cause and effect; the mode and the substance, the design and the execution, and active and never ceasing operator.

The existence of man is essentially connected with this vast whole, and it is impossible that he should ever detach any part of himself from the immortal system of which he forms a component part. The intervolutions of matter with matter, are universal and eternal; the essence of which man is composed, will therefore eternize its reciprocal relation with the vast fabric of material substance, which is presented to intelligent beings

---

[1] Some of the remarks herein contained are taken from the manuscript of a philosophic friend.

throughout the regions of space. A comprehensive view of the energies and relations of the material world, would, no doubt, shake to the centre the theological absurdities of antiquity; but it would leave to contemplative man the high consolation of having discovered from what source he originated, and to what destination the unalterable laws of nature have devoted his existence.

The highest intellectual joy consists in the discovery of truth; a knowledge of this truth will constantly tend to the practice of an exalted virtue; this virtue will serve as the stable foundation of human happiness, the immortal guarantee of the felicity of the intelligent world. Reason anticipates a progress, which all the powers of superstition can never arrest. Let reason then perform her faithful duty, and ignorance, fanaticism, and misery, will be banished from the earth. A new age, the true millennium will then commence; the standard of truth and of science will then be erected among the nations of the world, and man, the unlimited proprietor of his own person, may applaud himself in the result of his energies, and contemplate with indescribable satisfaction the universal improvement and happiness of the human race.

A Select Bibliography

Aldridge, Alfred Owen, *Man of Reason: The Life of Thomas Paine* (1959).

Aner, Karl, *Die Theologie der Lessingzeit* (1929).

Bredvold, Louis I., *The Intellectual Milieu of John Dryden* (1934).

Bury, J. B., *The Idea of Progress* (1920).

Carré, Meyrick H., tr. and ed., *De veritate, by Edward, Lord Herbert of Cherbury* (1937).

Cassirer, Ernst, *The Philosophy of the Enlightenment* (1932; tr. 1951).

Chadwick, Henry, tr. and ed., *Lessing's Theological Writings* (1957).

Colligan, J. Hay, *The Arian Movement in England* (1913).

Cragg, G. R., *From Puritanism to the Age of Reason: A Study of Changes in Religious Thought within the Church of England, 1660-1700* (1950).

Creed, John Martin, and John Sandwith Boys Smith, eds., *Religious Thought in the Eighteenth Century, Illustrated from Writers of the Period* (1934).

Dilthey, Wilhelm, "Lessing," in *Das Erlebnis und die Dichtung* (ed. 1922).

Gay, Peter, *The Enlightenment: An Interpretation,* vol. I, *The Rise of Modern Paganism* (1966).

————, *The Party of Humanity: Essays in the French Enlightenment* (1964).

————, *Voltaire's Politics: The Poet as Realist* (1959).

Harrison, A. W., *Arminianism* (1937).

Hazard, Paul, *European Thought in the Eighteenth Century* (1946; tr. 1954).

Lantoine, Albert, *Un précurseur de la Franc-maçonnerie: John Toland, 1670-1722* (1927).

Lovejoy, Arthur O., *The Great Chain of Being* (1936).

————, "The Parallel of Deism and Classicism," *Essays in the History of Ideas* (1948).

McLachlan, H. John, *Socinianism in Seventeenth-Century England* (1951).

Miller, Perry, *Jonathan Edwards* (1949).

Morais, Herbert M., *Deism in Eighteenth Century America* (1934).

Mossner, Ernest C., *Bishop Butler and the Age of Reason* (1936).
——, *The Life of David Hume* (1954).

Orr, John, *English Deism: Its Roots and Fruits* (1934).

Palmer, Robert R., *Catholics and Unbelievers in Eighteenth Century France* (1939).

Pattison, Mark, *Essays,* 2 vols., ed. H. Nettleship (1889).

Pomeau, René, *La religion de Voltaire* (1956).

Schmidt, E., *Lessings Leben und Werke,* 2 vols. (2nd ed., 1899).

Stephen, Sir Leslie, *A History of English Thought in the Eighteenth Century,* 2 vols. (1876; 3rd ed., 1902).

Strauss, D. F., *Hermann Samuel Reimarus und seine Schutzschrift für die vernünftigen Verehrer Gottes* (1862).

Stromberg, Roland N., *Religious Liberalism in Eighteenth-Century England* (1954).

Sykes, Norman, *Church and State in England in the Eighteenth Century* (1934).

Torrey, Norman L., *Voltaire and the English Deists* (1930).

Tulloch, John, *Rational Theology and Christian Philosophy in England in the Seventeenth Century,* 2 vols. (1872).

Voltaire (François-Marie Arouet), *Philosophical Dictionary,* 2 vols. ed. and tr. Peter Gay (1962).
——, *Sermon of the Fifty,* ed. and tr. J. A. R. Séguin (1962).

VAN NOSTRAND ANVIL BOOKS already published